This research was funded for two years by a grant from The Scottish Office Home and Health Department. The views expressed in the Report are entirely those of the authors.

PREFACE

The police investigation of crimes of violence against women and children is an area which, as this report demonstrates, has seen rapid changes in police policy and practice in recent years. As a consequence, some of the information contained in the report may already be out of date.

Since the completion of the fieldwork for the research there have been a number of new developments, particularly in the recruitment and training of staff for the Units. For example, Lothian and Borders have now introduced male officers into their Units; in Central appointment to the Unit is now by application, interview and a three month attachment as an `aide'. Lothian and Borders now provide regular input on child protection and serious sexual offences into police probationer and refresher courses and there is an initial training course for potential Unit members attended by both female and male officers. The joint training of police officers and their social work counterparts is also more widespread.

The rapid growth of specialist Units over the last ten years is recorded in this report. There will, without doubt, be further developments and changes in their structure, remit and staffing and the way in which they are percieved within individual Force areas and the police as a whole.

September 1993

ACKNOWLEDGEMENTS

This research would not have been possible without the granting of access by the Association of Chief Police Officers (Scotland) and we wish to thank the Chief Constables of the eight Scottish Forces for agreeing to participate.

We are indebted to the many officers in all Forces who gave us their time and invaluable assistance throughout the period of the research. Their continuing cooperation was essential for the successful completion of the work.

We would particularly like to thank the specialist officers who meticulously filled in data collection forms, participated in lengthy interviews and made time to explain police procedures and answer queries for the research.

We would also like to thank the regional Social Work Departments which gave us access to their staff and all the social workers who participated in interviews.

Thanks are also due to the voluntary agencies and support groups who took the time to fill in and return our questionnaire.

Dorothy Harcus undertook a large number of social work interviews and we thank her for her assistance. Vivienne Riddoch entered information from the data collection exercise onto the computer, and Edwin van Teijlingen gave vaulable advice and assistance in processing the data. Karen Stewart, Departmental Secretary in the Sociology Department helped with the production of the final report. Our thanks to them all.

Finally we thank the Research Secretary, Heather Wilson, for conscientiously and efficiently undertaking a wide range of secretarial and administrative tasks over the last two years. For her patience and skill in producing this report we give her sincere thanks.

Michele Burman and Siobhan Lloyd
Aberdeen
November 1992

CONTENTS

LIST OF TABLES

ABBREVIATIONS USED IN THE REPORT

ACC   Assistant Chief Constable
CAFSES   Child and Female Specialist Enquiry Section
CIB   Community Involvement Branch
CID   Criminal Investigation Department
CON   Constable
CPU   Child Protection Unit
DC   Detective Constable
DCI   Detective Chief Inspector
DCS   Detective Chief Superintendent
DI   Detective Inspector
DS   Detective Sergeant
DSUP   Detective Superintendent
FACU   Female and Child Unit
FO   Force Orders
WACU   Woman and Child Unit
INSP   Inspector
PF   Procurator Fiscal
RCC   Rape Crisis Centre
SGT   Sergeant
SUP   Superintendent
SWD   Social Work Department
VSS   Victim Support Scheme
WPC   Woman Police Constable

EXECUTIVE SUMMARY

1. Introduction

1.1 The last twenty years have seen much public concern with the difficulties experienced by women reporting sexual assault to the police and the subsequent investigation of such crimes. More recently, the increased reporting of child abuse has led to a questioning of the appropriateness of traditional police methods of investigation for child victims.

1.2 In response to public calls for changes and the issuing of guidelines from The Scottish Office, all eight Scottish police Forces have introduced new strategies aimed at improving the investigation of crimes of violence against women and children. This report provides an overview of the changes in policy and practice of police methods of investigation in each Force based on information from Force visits, an analysis of policy documents, the monitoring of a sample of investigations and interviews with police policy makers, specialist officers and social workers.

2 Specialist Units and specialist officers

2.1 Between 1984 and 1991, five Forces set up specialist Female and Child Units staffed by teams of officers with a remit to assist the CID in the investigation of sexual assault of women and child abuse (Strathclyde, Lothian and Borders, Tayside, Grampian and Dumfries and Galloway. One Force (Northern) deployed specialist officers throughout the Force who, in addition to other duties, assist in sexual assault and child abuse investigations. Two Forces (Central and Fife), established teams of officers in Child Protection Units who investigate child abuse jointly with designated social workers.

2.2 Officers are seconded to the Units for a specified 2-3 year period. In all Units except Grampian and the two Child Protection Units, the specialist officers are female. All are plain-clothed.

2.3 Specialist Units represent a more unified approach to investigations, although there is wide variation between Forces in terms of each Unit's remit, responsibilities and model of working.

2.4 Specialist officers provide care and support for victims. Some Units deal with the full range of sexual crimes and forms of child abuse: others deal with a more restricted range of offences.

2.5 The nature of the working relationship between the Units and the CID differs from Force to Force. In some Forces, specialist officers undertake the entire investigation, in others officers deal with the victim only.

2.6 Domestic violence is not part of the remit of the specialist Units.

2.7 Six Forces have established dedicated facilities used solely for the interviewing of victims of sexual assault and child abuse. The 'interview suites' provide, for the most part, a secure and private environment for victims although the location of some 'suites' within police stations could be improved.

| 2.8 | In five Forces, interview suites have adjoining fully-equipped medical examination facilities which allow examinations to take place in a clinical environment. |

2.8   In five Forces, interview suites have adjoining fully-equipped medical examination facilities which allow examinations to take place in a clinical environment.

2.9   In most Forces, specialist officers have to rely on other police officers or social workers for transport.

3.   <u>Victim-centred investigations</u>

3.1   A specialist officer is responsible for providing care and support to the victim throughout the investigation. The welfare of sexual assault victims has a higher priority in police investigations than a decade ago. The specialist officer elicits the victim's statement, accompanies the woman throughout all police procedures, and acts as a contact point thereafter. It is now unlikely for a victim to have to repeat details of the allegation to several officers, the investigation is conducted more swiftly, only essential procedures are carried out in the initial stages of the investigation and more detailed questioning takes place once the victim has rested.

3.2   In child abuse investigations most children are interviewed only once and interviews are more victim-centred. The police have refined their interviewing skills and have become more concerned with child protection.

3.3   Specialist officers recorded their involvement in a total of 898 inquiries during a four month study period. Of these, 136 (15%) were reports of sexual assaults of adult women. Allegations of rape accounted for exactly half of all reports of adult sexual assault; indecent assaults accounted for just over one quarter of reports; attempted rapes 15% and assaults with intent to ravish accounted for 9%.

3.4   Child abuse accounts for approximately four-fifths of investigations undertaken within the Units; sexual assault investigations, together with a small amount of other types of investigations such as receiving indecent mail and telephone calls, cot deaths and missing persons enquiries account for the remainder.

3.5   Increased levels of reporting, especially of child abuse cases, have resulted in a high volume of work. In most Forces, Units are stretched to capacity, with officers having to balance priorities when working simultaneously on a number of investigations. This heavy workload has implications for the future remit of the Units.

3.6   In 28% of cases, children underwent a second interview. Medical examinations were carried out in 42% of cases, most of which involved allegation of sexual abuse.

3.7   Specialist officers did not display such intense pre-occupations with the complainer's credibility as did the officers interviewed for research in the early 1980's. All officers stated that they did not take the demeanour of women reporting assault as an indicator of distress or veracity.

3.8   False reporting of sexual assault was not thought by specialist officers to be common.

3.9   Seventeen of the eighteen officers interviewed stated that their main function was to gather evidence. Giving care and support to the victim was seen as a secondary function.

4   Provision of information

4.1   Information to victims   about the progress of investigations remains patchy and leaves room for improvement.

4.2   Although all Units give talks and presentations about their work to other agencies and community groups, it can be difficult for members of the public to make direct contact with the Units.

5.   Joint investigations

5.1   In most Forces joint interviews with social workers for child abuse investigations are increasingly the norm, although there is much variation between and within Forces. The extent and degree of joint working is dependent on a range of factors, some of which relate to the organisational context within which the investigation takes place; others relate to the stage of development reached on joint working in individual Forces.

5.2   The inception of the Units has signalled an increase in knowledge between social work and police about their respective roles, practice, organisational constraints and statutory responsibilities. Professional conflict, especially in relation to the timing and direction of an interview with a child is evident, but there have been improvements in the amount of information shared between the two agencies.

6.   Trained officers

6.1   All Forces have developed a specific training strategy for specialist officers, although there is variation between Forces in the structure, context, quantity and quality of that training. Many courses aim to develop sensitive interviewing techniques and they include information on the impact of sexual violence on the victim.   In general, training is participative and skills-based, using role-playing, simulated interviews and case studies. There is greater willingness in some Forces for contributions from outside speakers and voluntary agencies which provide support to victims.

6.2   In most Forces, officers attend multi-disciplinary training sessions. This has widened the parameters of police training in child abuse and it has given officers the opportunity to meet with other child protection professionals in their geographical area.

6.3   There is scope for more training on a number of topics, including the interviewing of children who are young, disturbed or disabled.

7   Relations with other agencies

7.1   The investigation of child abuse, in particular, has brought the police into a clearer working relationship with other professionals involved in child protection.

7.2   Working relationships with social workers vary between and within Forces, depending on the extent of joint working that takes place. In some Forces, 'exchange systems' have been established whereby officers and social workers swap workplaces to gain inside experience and knowledge of each others' roles and responsibilities in relation to child protection.

7.3   Relationships with Procurators Fiscal and Reporters have improved on both an agency and an individual basis. Relationships with police surgeons vary and leave room for improvement.

7.4   In some Forces, there has been an improvement in relations with support and counselling agencies in the voluntary sector.

8   The work of the Units

8.1   The most enjoyable and rewarding aspect of the work of the specialist officers were identified as: heightened responsibility; the opportunity to plan an investigative strategy; being able to see an investigation through to the end; working as part of a team and the development of improved working relations with other professionals.

8.2   The heavy workload was cited as one of the most difficult aspects of the work. The organisation of the work was felt to be more stressful than the nature of the investigations. A minority of officers referred to feelings of stress at some time since working in the Units. They have little access to support or counselling services.

8.3   Two-thirds of officers felt that their work was seen as low priority by other officers.

CHAPTER 1

RESEARCH AIMS AND METHODOLOGY

1.1 INTRODUCTION

The last two decades have witnessed an increase in public awareness of the issue of violence against women and children. The professional response to adult sexual assault and child abuse has come under close scrutiny and there has been growing concern about the way in which victims of these crimes are treated by the police, the courts and other statutory agencies. Police conduct in the investigation of such crimes has been the subject of criticism from a variety of sources. Scottish Office guidance concerning the police investigation of sexual assault was issued in 1976 and in 1985,[1] and on the handling of domestic violence in 1990.[2] In 1989, official guidance was issued to all agencies involved in child protection, calling for a multi-agency approach to child abuse investigations.[3] From the mid-1980s onwards, Scottish police authorities introduced new strategies aimed at improving policing in these much-criticised areas. This study focuses on the police initiative of specialist Units set up for the investigation of crimes of violence against women and children.

1.2 AIMS AND SCOPE OF THE RESEARCH

The purpose of this research was to examine the organisation, objectives and operation of the specialist Units. The broad aim was to ascertain the nature and extent of the changes in policy and practice of police methods of investigation represented by the Units. The research also sought to assess on the one hand, the degree of liaison and co-operation developed and maintained between the Units and Social Work Departments (SWDs), the other key agency involved in the investigation of child abuse; and on the other the relationship between the Units and voluntary organisations offering support to women and children who have suffered violence.

The research had three main objectives. The first objective was to examine the motivation for changes in policing policy and practice, and the research set out to chart the events and developments that led to the inception of the Units. This involved identifying the impetus for these developments within each Force. It also involved looking at how each Force interpreted and responded to the official guidelines on police investigation of sexual assault and child abuse.

This information was important for the second research objective, which was to examine the way in which policy directives were disseminated and put into practice within each Force.

The third objective was to examine aspects of working practice in the Units. Here, the research focused on the processing of sexual assault allegations and child abuse referrals by officers in the Units. Information was sought on the volume and type of investigations handled by the Units, the procedure followed during investigations, the investigative methods utilised and the nature of the contact with other agencies during and after investigations.

The research did not have a remit to report on the subjective experiences of women reporting sexual assault, nor of children who were the subject of child abuse investigations conducted by officers in the Units. Nor, unfortunately, was it possible to provide a fully documented national comparison of investigative practice before the inception of the Units. However, two key studies provide information on the situation in some Scottish Forces prior to the inception of the Units and they were important points of reference. _Investigating Sexual Assault_[4] gave a graphic description of the police investigation and processing of reports of rape and rape-related offences by adult women in two Scottish cities in the early 1980s. *Child Sexual Abuse: The Professional Challenge*[5] examined the way in which intra-familial child sexual abuse was identified and responded to by the professional services of four Scottish regions. Both studies are referred to extensively throughout this Report.

1.3 TIMING OF THE RESEARCH

Although the first Unit was set up by Strathclyde Police in 1984 they are, on the whole, relatively recent initiatives in Scotland. Many are still in the process of consolidating their remit and refining their practice. During the period of the research a number of significant changes took place: one Force set up their first Unit; new interview suites were opened in other Forces; the numbers of specialist officers allocated to existing Units grew; training programmes were modified and new training courses were introduced; aspects of working practice were refined and, most significantly, there were changes in the types of crimes and offences dealt with by some Units. All of these developments provided excellent opportunities to study the implementation and impact of policy changes on police practice, and the research was considerably enriched by being able to plot the emergence of new Units and the changes that took place within existing ones.

1.4 RESEARCH METHODS

The research design combined several different methods of information gathering. A research strategy was devised to ensure that each component built on and was informed by earlier stages of the work.

1.4.1 Fieldwork

Intensive periods of fieldwork were undertaken in all eight Scottish police Forces. Field visits were made to dedicated Units, interview suites and medical examination facilities. During the field visits, information was sought from police managers and Unit officers on the day-to-day operation of the Units and conduct of investigations. Policy and practice documents were collected. Observations were made of meetings between police managers and investigating officers and of strategy discussions between police and social workers. A joint training programme for police and social workers on the investigation of child abuse was observed.

Outwith the periods of fieldwork, contact with the police was maintained by regular telephone calls, letters and meetings. This high level of contact proved essential, not only for the maintenance of good working relations, but also because of changes in police personnel and expansion and change in the Units in all Forces.

1.4.2 Documentary analysis

A review of the statutory framework for investigations and the written policy within each Force was undertaken. A wide range of policy and practice documents from police Forces and SWDs were scrutinised. These included minutes of police/social work meetings, letters, stated objectives and policy statements of Units, Force Orders, Standing Orders, instructional memoranda, social work practice guidelines, training manuals, reports, staffing criteria and job descriptions. Investigation forms, case report forms, information retrieval systems, Unit log-books and daily diaries were also examined.

1.4.3 Data collection exercise

A data collection form,the SPU/1 form, was devised to record allegations and referrals. It was piloted for six weeks by Grampian Police, and then implemented in all Forces for a four-month period between July and October 1991.

For every case of sexual assault or child abuse dealt with by a specialist Unit, a form was filled in by the allocated specialist officer. The forms recorded the type and incidence of reports and referrals and basic details about the complainer, the perpetrator (if known), the nature of the allegation, the investigative process, the police interview, the medical examination and, where possible, the outcome of the investigation.

The forms were coded and analysed using the SSPX computer package.

1.4.4 Interviews

Police: Interviews were undertaken with twelve senior police officers responsible for the development of policy and the setting up of the Units. Four of these officers held the rank of Detective Chief Inspector (DCI), two were Detective Chief Superintendents (DCSs), two were Detective Superintendents (DSUPs), three were Superintendents (SUPs) and one was an Assistant Chief Constable (ACC). Eleven of these twelve officers were male. The interviews addressed the developments within each Force which led to the inception of the Units, liaison with other agencies, aims and objectives of the Units, management and organisational structure and decisions regarding remit, resources, training, staffing and siting of Units.

A second set of interviews were undertaken with a sample of eighteen officers from specialist Units across Scotland who were operationally involved in investigations. Two were Sergeants (SGTs), nine were Detective Constables (DCs) and seven were Constables (CONs). Seventeen of these officers were female (see Appendix 3). The interviews addressed aspects of police work, the investigation of allegations and referrals, their perception of the role and work of the Units, working relationships with other agencies, training issues and the effects of working in the Units.

Finally, interviews were held with officers responsible for training Unit personnel in four Forces. These were a Detective Inspector (DI), an Inspector (INSP), a Detective Sergeant (DS), and a Sergeant (SGT). Three of these officers were female. The interviews covered Force policy regarding training needs of Unit staff, the structure and content of courses, the training input given by other agencies and police input into other agencies' training.

Social workers: Twenty eight social workers from nine local authorities across Scotland were interviewed (Borders, Central, Dumfries and Galloway, Fife, Grampian, Highland, Lothian, Strathclyde and Tayside). Focusing on the work of the Units, these interviews were primarily concerned with police/social work relations in the investigation of child abuse. Police/social work relations in the context of sexual assault of adult women were not specifically addressed, unless the social worker had direct involvement with the police and a woman reporting sexual assault.

Ten of those interviewed were social work managers (Depute Directors, Assistant Directors, Principal Officers and Area Managers). Eight were male and two were female. These interviews addressed social work policy with regard to the Units in each region, organisational issues affecting joint working, their professional relationship with their police counterpart, information-sharing between police and social work and joint training issues. Eighteen were field social workers (Basic Grade Social Workers, Senior Social Workers and Senior Practitioners (Child Protection)) of whom twelve were female and six were male. Interviews with field social workers sought information on police/social work operational practice in child abuse investigations in the Units. Issues such as police/social work notification mechanisms, investigative procedure, information-sharing systems, roles, organisational structure and the effects of the Unit on social work practice were discussed.

The majority of police and social worker interviews were tape-recorded. Interview data was analysed by examining the transcripts and performing a simple content analysis, whereby responses were grouped together in terms of dominant themes. All interviewees have been anonymised in this report.

1.4.5 Postal Questionnaire

A postal questionnaire was sent to twenty-seven agencies which offer support or advice to survivors of sexual assault or child abuse. The majority of these were voluntary organisations. They included Rape Crisis Centres (RCC), Victim Support Schemes (VSS), Women's Aid Groups (WAID), local authority support and counselling schemes, ethnic minority support groups, Childline and the RSSPCC. There was a response rate of 81% with twenty-two agencies returning completed questionnaires.

The questionnaires sought information on the nature and quality of the professional contact between voluntary agencies and the Unit(s) in their region. Questions covered the agency's knowledge of and involvement with the Units, the type and the frequency of contact between the Units and the agency and arrangements regarding referrals of women and children to and from the Units.

The research strategy provided a wealth of data. Only the main issues and themes to emerge from the research are addressed in this Report.

Footnotes

1   CC Circular 1976: Investigation of Allegations of Rape. SHHD. CC Circular 7/1985: Investigation of Complaints of Sexual Assault. SHHD.
2   CC Circular 3/1990: Investigation of Complaints of Domestic Assault. SHHD.
3   Effective Intervention: Child Abuse - Guidance on Co-operation in Scotland. (1989) Social Work Services Group, Scottish Office.
4   Chambers, G. and Millar, A. (1983) Investigating Sexual Assault. HMSO.
5   Waterhouse, L. and Carnie, J. (1990), Child Sexual Abuse: The Professional Challenge. Report to Social Work Services Group, Scottish Office.

CHAPTER 2

KEY FINDINGS FROM THE RESEARCH

CHAPTER 4: FORMULATION OF POLICE POLICY

This Chapter outlines the main factors which affected the formulation of policy in each Force.

1. Scottish Forces responded differently to calls for change in the police investigation of crimes of violence against women and children. In some Forces the focus of change initially concerned the investigation of adult sexual assault and then extended to child abuse. Other Forces focused exclusively on the investigation of child abuse.

2. The point when individual Forces began to review their policies was important in accounting for the type of response. In the late 1980s there was a shift in emphasis from adult sexual assault to child abuse.

3. In each Force, a range of factors affected the formulation of policy. These included size of Force area, personnel, available resources and population size.

4. Other factors were more Force-specific. They included the attitude and motivation of individual policy-makers mandated to put forward new strategies in each Force; existing relationships with other agencies, especially Social Work Departments (SWDs) and internal Force administrative, organisational and staffing concerns.

5. Ten of the twelve policy-makers interviewed felt changes in the police response to sexual assault had been needed, two did not.

6. Six policy-makers referred to the need for caution and scepticism when dealing with reports of sexual assault and child abuse.

7. The provision of a "professional response" was an underlying concern of most policy-makers. One third viewed specialist Units as a means of consolidating the role of women police officers.

8. Increased levels of reporting of child abuse was an important factor prompting reformulation of policy. The police perspective shifted from a concern with prosecution to incorporate a concern with the protection of the child.

9. Internal reviews of existing arrangements for the investigation of crimes of violence against women and children took place in all Forces.

10. In most cases, the period of research and review that pre-dated policy revisions was extensive, and involved visits to other initiatives in England and consultation with other statutory agencies such as Procurators Fiscal, Reporters, SWDs and health authorities.

11. A small number of Forces sought views from voluntary support organisations and women's groups.

12. The focus of policy revision was victim rather than offender-linked.

13. The establishment of specialist Units represents a more unified approach to crimes of violence against women and children, although there has been wide variation across Forces in terms of each Unit's remit, responsibilities and the model of working which they adopted.

14. Several Forces have updated their Force Orders since the inception of the Units to reflect changes in staff numbers, deployment and additional facilities.

CHAPTER 5: ORGANISATIONAL STRUCTURE AND THE DEPLOYMENT OF SPECIALIST OFFICERS.

This Chapter outlines the way in which Units are organised and staffed.

15. Five Forces (Dumfries and Galloway, Grampian, Lothian and Borders, Strathclyde and Tayside) deployed teams of specialist officers in dual-responsibility Units with a remit for the investigation of sexual assault and child abuse. The Units were established at different times, the first (Strathclyde) in 1984, the most recent (Dumfries & Galloway) in 1991. These Units are staffed by police only.

16. Two Forces (Central in 1989 and Fife in 1990) established teams of specialist officers in Child Protection Units (CPUs). The Units focus exclusively on the investigation of child abuse. Formal joint working arrangements exist with regional SWDs. In Central CPU, officers undertake investigations with designated social workers in social work area offices. In Fife CPU, police and social workers are based in and work together from one centralised location.

17. Northern is the only Force which does not have specialist teams of officers deployed in Units. Women officers from the uniform and Community Involvement Branch (CIB) are trained in the investigation of sexual assault and child abuse. They undertake these investigations in addition to their other duties. There are plans to establish specialist Units in this Force in the future.

18. In Forces where there is more than one Unit, a 'main' Unit forms a centralised base overseeing the work of 'satellite' Units in other Divisions. The exception is Strathclyde where Divisional Units operate on a localised basis.

19. There are clear advantages to having promoted officers (SGTs or DSs) heading specialist teams of officers, in terms of the identity of the Unit, the even distribution of work and dealing with day to day problems.

20. In all Units except Grampian and the two CPUs, the specialist officers are female. All are plain clothed.

21. With the exception of the CPUs, officers are given little choice about secondment to the Units.

22. Length of secondment to the Units differs in each Force. Initially most Forces set this at three years, but recently the trend is for a secondment of two to two and a half years.

23. Units function as operational arms of the CID, and all except the Unit in Tayside are accountable to the CID. The Unit in Tayside is accountable to the Community Involvement Branch.

24. Most specialist officers are seconded from the uniform Branch of the police. In four Forces, specialist officers are designated CID for the duration of their secondment. This has led to some animosity from other officers.

25. Working hours in the Units differ from Force to Force. Some Units operate a standard police shift system; others have weekday working hours of 9 am to 5 pm.

26. In some Units only one officer is on duty per shift. In some cases there is no overlap between shifts for the 'handing over' of work.

27. Six of the eight Forces have established 'dedicated facilities' for the interviewing of victims. Not all of these 'interview suites' are equipped with medical examination facilities.

28. In most Forces, specialist officers have to rely on CID officers or social workers for transport. Lack of vehicles can often impede their work.

29. Most Units give talks and presentations about their work to other agencies and community groups.

30. Little is known by other officers about the nature and amount of work undertaken by Unit officers. Notification of cases is made to Units via channels other than police radio or central control room.

31. It can be difficult for the public to make direct contact with the Units.

CHAPTER 6: WOMEN OFFICERS AND THE INVESTIGATION OF SEXUAL ASSAULT AND CHILD ABUSE

This Chapter considers the high incidence of women specialist officers.

32. The nature of the work undertaken by specialist officers resembles that done in the 'policewomen's departments' which existed before the Sex Discrimination Act 1975.

33. In some Forces, specialist training and secondment to a Unit is mandatory for all post-probation women officers.

34. Work with women and child victims is seen within the police as 'women's work' rather than 'real' policing.

35. The Units represent one means of mobilising women officers into areas for which they are perceived to be more suited than male officers.

CHAPTER 7: TRAINING FOR SPECIALIST OFFICERS

This Chapter outlines the training provisions which have been developed for specialist officers.

36.   All Forces have a specific training strategy for specialist officers, although there is variation between Forces in the structure, content, quantity and quality of that training.

37.   Training can be grouped into four main categories:
- serious sexual offences courses (attended by police only)
- serious sexual offences and child abuse courses (attended by police only)
- joint training on child abuse investigations (attended by police and social workers)
- multi-disciplinary training sessions on child abuse (attended by professionals from a range of child protection agencies).

In all Forces specialist officers attend at least one of the above types of training.

38.   Across Forces specialist officers undergo training for work in the Units at different points either before, during or after their secondment.

39.   Many training courses now go considerably beyond the relevant legislation, legal-evidential requirements, medical and forensic matters relating to sexual assault and child abuse; they include the development of interviewing skills and information on the impact of sexual violence on the victim.

40.   Training is now rarely conducted by means of lectures.   It is more participative and skills-based, and includes methods such as role-playing, simulated interviews and hypothetical case studies.   The influence of social work training methods is evident in the structure, content and methods of training.   Officers welcome the variety of methods now used.

41.   There is a greater willingness in some Forces to bring in outside speakers and to give a voice to voluntary agencies which provide support to victims.

42.   Multi-disciplinary training sessions provide a valuable forum for specialist officers to meet other child protection professionals.   They have widened the parameters of police training in child abuse and are positively viewed by officers.

43.   In some Forces 'aide systems' have been established whereby potential specialist officers are given the opportunity to experience the work of the Units for a period prior to secondment.   Officers welcome these developments.

44.   In some Forces 'exchange systems' have been established whereby specialist officers and social workers swap workplaces to gain valuable inside experience and knowledge of each others' roles and responsibilities in relation to child protection officers.

45.   Half of the officers found police-only courses beneficial.

46.   There was a range of views on joint police/social work training. The main advantages were perceived to be: learning more about the social work role, learning new skills for interviewing children and building trust.

CHAPTER 8: THE ROLE AND FUNCTION OF SPECIALIST OFFICERS

This Chapter draws together the information from previous Chapters as an introduction to a description of the operation of the Units.

47.   Specialist officers provide care and support for victims. Some Units deal with the full range of sexual crimes (eg. rape, indecent assault, under-age sex, indecent exposure) and forms of child abuse (sexual, physical, neglect); others deal with a more restricted range of offences.

48.   The nature of the working relationship between the Units and the CID differs from Force to Force. In some Forces specialist officers undertake the entire investigation, including the apprehension of the suspect. In others, specialist officers deal with the victim only, giving assistance to the CID officer who is responsible for handling the investigation in terms of the detection of the offender and the reporting of the case to the Procurator Fiscal.

49.   In general, the degree of involvement of specialist officers in investigations depends on the type of crime being reported and its perceived seriousness.

50.   Domestic violence is not part of the remit of the specialist Units, although a 'domestic violence initiative' is currently being undertaken by one Unit in Strathclyde. This will assess the feasibility of Units responding to incidents of domestic violence.

51.   In some Forces the duties of specialist officers extend to dealing with cot deaths, 'vulnerable' witnesses in other types of crimes and missing persons. Unofficial duties may include accompanying female suspects during various police procedures and entering data onto the police computer.

CHAPTER 9: THE INVESTIGATION OF SEXUAL ASSAULT

This Chapter describes police action following the report of a sexual assault.

52.   Specialist officers recorded their involvement in a total of 898 enquiries during a four month period. 136 (15%) of these were reports of sexual assaults of adult women.

53.   Allegations of rape accounted for exactly half of all reports of adult sexual assault. Indecent assaults accounted for just over a quarter (26%) of reports, attempted rape for 15%, and assault with intent to ravish accounted for 9%.

54. All Forces have mechanisms for notifying Units whenever a report of sexual assault is made to the police. Most Force instructions emphasise the requirement that Units are notified of a sexual assault as soon as possible.

55. Allocation of cases is done on the basis of existing workload or by means of a rota system.

56. Once allocated, the specialist officer remains attached to the case and is responsible for providing support to the complainer and assisting the CID throughout all enquiries. The allocation of one officer is aimed at reducing the number of officers coming into contact with the complainer and her having to repeat the allegations to different officers.

57. Most reports (59%) were made during the late evening or early hours of the morning. In 63% of cases the women contacted local police directly.

58. Initial contact is likely to be with uniformed police. Specialist officers dealt with 52% of women within one hour of contacting the police (this included 64% of rape reports). 21% made contact between one and two hours after reporting; 14% between two and four hours; 13% made contact the next day.

59. The majority of specialist officers recognise the importance of the early stages of an investigation for establishing rapport with a woman. Fifteen of the eighteen specialist officers prefaced the interview with an introduction which explained police procedures and assured anonymity. Specialist officers are alert to the needs of women reporting sexual assault. There is an emphasis on the building of trust to facilitate a smoother investigation and reduce the trauma for the complainer.

60. There are two stages in an investigation. The first usually involves the initial statement, a visit to the scene of crime and the medical examination. The second may involve taking a fuller statement and other police procedures such as photographing injuries, an identification parade and looking at photographs for a possible perpetrator. The specialist officer accompanies the woman throughout all these procedures.

61. Information regarding the allegation is relayed by the specialist officer to the CID investigating officer.

62. Medical examinations were conducted in 41% of sexual assault cases. The specialist officer was present during the examination and had responsibility for the care of material evidence. The majority of examinations took place in a hospital, doctor's surgery or the medical room in an interview suite; 15% took place in police offices.

63. The complainer is usually allowed to go home after being medically examined, unless there are any other essential procedures to complete such as finger-printing and photographing injuries.

64. In 34% of cases, the first stage of the investigation took up to an hour, 28% took between one and two hours and 38% took over two hours.

65. The statement interview is undertaken by the specialist officer in private with the woman. Several officers were 'territorial' about this part of the investigation and were reluctant to allow the CID investigating officer access to question the woman.

66. Specialist officers did not display such intense preoccupations with the complainer's credibility as the officers interviewed by Chambers and Millar (1983). All officers stated that they did not take the demeanour of women reporting assault as an indicator of her distress or the veracity of her account.

67. False reporting of sexual assault was not thought by specialist officers to be common.

68. In most Forces, information leaflets describing the procedures following a report of sexual assault are given to complainers. They are also given general information about medical, social work, housing and support agencies.

69. The provision of information to complainers concerning progress with the case continues to be unsystematic and variable.

CHAPTER 10: WORKING RELATIONSHIPS WITH VOLUNTARY ORGANISATIONS

This Chapter considers working relationships between the Units and voluntary organisations which offer support to women and children.

70. In general, voluntary support agencies see the Units as a considerable improvement on prior police practice in the investigation of sexual assault. Interview suites providing privacy and security and the availability of trained and informed women officers are particularly welcome.

71. Voluntary agencies see a number of disadvantages to the Units. They include restricted skill development in male officers (due to the predominance of women officers in such work); the marginalisation of violence against women as these crimes are dealt with outside mainstream policing; a possible "standing back" by the rest of the Force because of a general perception that something is being done about violent crime against women and children.

CHAPTER 11: ARRANGEMENTS FOR THE INVESTIGATION OF CHILD ABUSE

This Chapter examines existing working arrangements for the investigation of child abuse by the Units and regional social work departments.

72. Joint working arrangements are under constant discussion and review by police and SWDs. The aim in all regions has been to establish more formalised joint procedures to be followed in most cases of child abuse.

73.   Several significant changes have occurred during a relatively short period. Some developments have occurred at a localised level and practice can differ within regions.

74.   There are major differences concerning the extent to which particular aspects of investigations are carried out jointly and whether these procedures are stated in agency guidelines or instructions.

75.   Not all allegations of abuse are passed on to the 'partner' agency. One important factor concerns the type of abuse and its degree of seriousness; a second relates to the type and quality of information received.

76.   In potentially serious cases of child abuse, each agency seeks the assistance of the other to lessen the chances of making a mistake and to share the burden of responsibility.

77.   Specialist officers dealt with 710 reports of child abuse during the four month data collection period. This accounted for 79% of their caseload.

78.   63% of child abuse cases were categorised as sexual abuse; 27% as physical abuse; 6% as neglect; and 4% as a combination of sexual and/or physical abuse and/or neglect.

79.   Two thirds of the victims were female; one third were male.

80.   In at least 35% of cases, other professionals had interviewed the child before notifying the police.

81.   67% of cases of child abuse were made known to the police during weekday working hours.

82.   A common concern of police and social workers related to differences in the quality and amount of information sought and exchanged at the outset of an investigation.

83.   There is an increased recognition of the value of early inter-agency discussion in order to determine an appropriate course of action.

84.   If a joint interview is agreed, a 'strategy meeting' takes place between police and social workers, during which they formulate a joint plan of action.

85.   Interviews with children were undertaken in 97% of cases dealt with by specialist officers. 37% of these were joint interviews.

86.   Police tend to lead in joint interviews except in areas where CPUs exist; in these areas police are happy for specialist social workers to take the lead.

87.	49% of interviews were undertaken in the child's home; 24% took place in an interview suite. The remainder took place in hospitals, schools and relatives' homes

88.	Two thirds of first interviews lasted between half an hour to two hours; only 2% took over four hours.

89.	In 28% of cases, children underwent a second interview.

90.	Medical examinations were carried out in 42% of cases. Most of these involved allegations of sexual abuse. 13% underwent a second medical and 1% underwent a third.

91.	Arrangements for the care of the child are seen by specialist officers as the responsibility of the SWD.

92.	In at least 44% of cases, a report was sent to the Procurator Fiscal.

93.	Police and social workers perceive the advantages of joint working to be: a child-centred approach; improved communication; access to more information; better planning; pooling of expertise; a learning experience; increased mutual trust and confidence; mutual support and sharing of responsibility.

94.	Impediments to joint working concern organisational issues such as hours of working; lack of resources; specialist Units working with generic social workers; different areas of jurisdiction (for example one Unit may work with several social work area offices). A second set of difficulties concern the incompatibility of roles and perspectives between some police officers and social workers.

95.	Differences in working relationships are due to a range of factors including the number of social work area offices with which a Unit may work and the frequency with which officers work together on investigations. In Lothian and Borders local variation is also the result of one Force working with two social work departments.

CHAPTER 12: THE VIEWS OF SPECIALIST OFFICERS

This Chapter gives a voice to the views held by specialist officers about the nature of their work.

96.	Most officers felt that dealing with sexual crimes and child abuse, due to their intimate and distressing nature, required a different police approach to other crimes and offences.

97.	Officers thought that child abuse and sexual assault cases shared three main similarities: the intimate nature of the offences; potential for trauma for the victim; the predominance of male perpetrators.

98. Despite some similarities in approach, the main differences between child abuse and sexual assault investigations were: joint working in child abuse cases meant investigations were carried out in a different organisational context; emphasis on the protection of children meant police were involved in decisions to remove a child; child abuse investigations required a different range of skills.

99. Officers spoke of having to "balance priorities" when working simultaneously on child abuse and sexual assault cases. Given the volume of work this can be very difficult.

100. Seventeen of the eighteen officers stated that their main function was to gather evidence. Giving care and support to the victim was a secondary function.

101. Three quarters of the specialist officers enjoy their work in the Units.

102. The most enjoyable and rewarding aspects of their work were identified as: heightened responsibility; the opportunity to plan an investigative strategy; being able to see an investigation through to the end; working as part of a team; the development of improved working relations with other professionals .

103. Two thirds of officers felt that working in the Units provided very valuable practical experience.

104. The heavy workload was cited as one of the most difficult aspects of the work. Officers felt that they received work which could be easily dealt with by other officers. They also felt that other officers were loathe to undertake child abuse and sexual assault enquiries.

105. The organisation of the work was felt to be more stressful than the nature of investigations. Common organisational difficulties included: arranging medical examinations; transportation problems; lack of interview facilities; different working hours to social workers; volume and organisation of paperwork.

106. Additional frustrations stemmed from difficulties in obtaining corroboration in sexual assault and child abuse cases.

107. Two-thirds of officers felt that their work was seen as low priority by other officers.

108. A minority of officers referred to feelings of stress at some time since working in the Units. They have little access to support or counselling services.

CHAPTER 3

GENERAL BACKGROUND

Specialist Units for the investigation of crimes of violence against women and children have emerged primarily in response to concerns about police handling of the investigation of sexual assault of women and child abuse. This Chapter traces the history of the Units in this context. Tables 3.1 and 3.2 list the publication of relevant reports and government guidelines in both areas.

3.1 DEVELOPMENTS IN THE POLICE RESPONSE TO SEXUAL ASSAULT

The last twenty years have seen a growing concern with the way in which the law and the criminal justice system treat women. One focus of this concern has been with the difficulties experienced by women reporting sexual assault and the way they are treated by the police. One specific criticism was that police were unwilling to believe that the woman was telling the truth.[1] Women reporting sexual assault to the police were treated insensitively, enquiries were conducted with little regard to the woman's well-being and women were subjected to excessively detailed questioning on their personal background and history.[2] This led to a public perception of the police investigation as an ordeal for women. In addition, because women are reluctant to report sexual assault, there are concerns that rape and other crimes of sexual violence are under-reported. Guilty offenders therefore evade prosecution.

The past fifteen years have also witnessed increased concern with the needs and rights of victims. The recognition of previously hidden forms of victimisation is partly the result of crime victimisation surveys which have provided alternatives to statistics on crime levels produced by the police. The British Crime Survey (Scotland) for example, has revealed that only 7% of sexual assaults were reported to the police.[3]

The women's movement has been instrumental in raising questions about male violence against women and children and the police response to it. Feminist critiques have also made the case for reform.[4] Rape Crisis Centres, women's support networks and counselling groups have been established in many areas, offering support and advice to women who have been sexually assaulted.

In early 1982, public awareness of the nature of the police response was heightened by the broadcasting of a television documentary which showed detectives in the Thames Valley Police responding to a report of rape and 'investigating' the woman who had made the report. In the public outcry which followed the programme, several Forces issued public statements disassociating themselves from the sort of practices depicted in the documentary.

The same year saw a number of other newsworthy events which focused further attention on the treatment of women in the criminal justice system. These included the 'hitchhiking' case in which the trial judge stated that the victim's 'contributory negligence' was a factor in her rape and he fined the offender £2,000. In the same year a Glasgow rape case, in which a case of a group rape where the complainer sustained severe injuries, was dropped on the grounds that the complainer was deemed unfit to go through a trial.[5]

In 1983, Chambers and Millar published *Investigating Sexual Assault*, a study of the police response to reports of rape and assault with intent to rape in two Scottish cities.[6] This was a highly critical study which verified the issues which had already been identified by women themselves. Four out of five women interviewed in the study reported distress at one or more aspects of the police investigation. They reported unfavourably on the attitudes of the police and the actual process of the investigation. Chambers and Millar pointed to a number of shortcomings in police practice. These included scepticism by police regarding reports of sexual assault; insensitive, relentless and repetitive questioning; complainers having to relate their account of what happened to different officers at different times; a general lack of consideration, for example leaving women to wait for long periods of time; discouraging women to continue with their case; inadequate and inappropriate facilities that lacked privacy and little information given to women about the progress of their case.

The report made recommendations in five areas:

- **General approach**: the well-being of the complainer should take a higher priority during the investigation. Only essential procedures would be carried out in the early stages after reporting and complainers would not be kept waiting for long periods.

- **Police training**: courses should be revised to include interviewing skills and material which provided insight into the meaning and impact of sexual violence for women.

- **Organisation of investigation**: enquiries in rape and sexual assault cases should be better organised and more thought given as to who should act as the enquiry officer in these cases. Specialist teams of officers should be considered to deal with such cases.

- **Medical examinations**: examinations should be conducted outwith police stations by doctors experienced in examining women who report sexual assault.

- **Providing assistance**: police could do more to reassure complainers that a sexual victimisation cannot be regarded as a woman's responsibility. Police should provide more information about the progress of the case.

In March 1983 The Home Office issued guidelines to Chief Police Officers in England and Wales on the police investigation of rape.[7] These guidelines recommended that investigating officers exercise tact and understanding in an atmosphere of care and concern, that women were told of local support agencies and that they were kept informed about any subsequent legal proceedings.

In 1985 The Scottish Office issued guidelines to Scottish Chief Constables on the investigation of sexual assault.[8] These guidelines referred explicitly to the report by Chambers and Millar and took up some of the recommendations of that study. The document mirrored the earlier guidance issued by The Home Office and referred to the following areas:

- The initial stage
- Medical examinations and treatment
- Further interviews
- Welfare of the complainer
- Anonymity of the complainer
- Follow-up action
- Police training.

The guidance emphasised the need for victims to be treated tactfully and sympathetically. It suggested that in-depth questioning of a personal nature should be avoided, that the privacy of the complainer should be maintained, that interviews should be conducted by trained officers designated for the purpose, that information about the progress of the case should be provided and that the complainer should be told of medical, social and voluntary services such as Rape Crisis Centres. There was also detailed guidance concerning medical examinations and the availability of police surgeons, encouraging the services of female doctors. There were, however, no recommendations for setting up specialist teams of officers as advocated by Chambers and Millar.

In December 1985, the Women's National Commission issued a report[9] which made a number of recommendations on the police handling of allegations of rape, sexual assault and domestic violence. This report recommended the deployment of officers in specialist teams to deal with sexual offences. It also called for improved training for uniformed and CID officers and for improvements in the police conduct of the investigation along the lines recommended by Chambers and Millar.

In 1986 The Home Office issued a further update on guidelines to Chief Officers in England and Wales.[10] It incorporated several of the recommendations made in the report by the WNC, notably a recognition of the value of specialist teams of female officers dealing exclusively with sexual offences against women and children. These guidelines also advocated the provision of special 'victim examination suites' where medical, toilet and interview facilities could be located in police offices 'away from the charge room and detention cells.'

More recent guidelines sent to Chief Constables in 1990 refer to the investigation of domestic violence.[11] They were introduced following campaigning by Women's Aid groups. The guidelines drew attention to the role of the police in ensuring the safety of victims and protecting children. They highlighted the need for a sympathetic and tactful approach by police and noted steps which could be taken to reassure victims, including giving them information about support agencies.

3.2   DEVELOPMENTS IN THE POLICE RESPONSE TO CHILD ABUSE

A series of events and developments over the last fifteen years have stimulated intensive examination of professional practice in child protection work. The late 1970s and early 1980s saw an increase in the visibility of child abuse as an issue of public and professional concern. Scrutiny of the professional handling of individual cases of child abuse and neglect uncovered deficiencies in existing child protection policies and procedures. Social workers in particular received much adverse criticism. Official reports and judicial enquiries into these cases repeatedly documented a lack of co-ordination and co-operation, poor communication, poor record-keeping and weaknesses in systems for information-sharing between agencies as major failings in the professional response.[12]

The Butler-Sloss Report[13] on events in Cleveland drew attention to shortcomings in the professional response to cases of suspected sexual abuse. It reiterated the main findings of earlier reports on physical abuse and neglect and strongly recommended increased interprofessional communication and understanding. Improvements in inter-agency co-operation were called for, along with joint policy objectives and better collaboration between agencies dealing with child abuse. The Report noted that close working relationships between police, health authorities and social work agencies were important in terms of assessment and intervention in cases of suspected sexual abuse. The training and support of staff were also seen as necessary for this work. The report prompted many local authorities to undertake reviews of their policy and practice in relation to child protection.

The report was followed by the publication of government guidance for inter-agency collaboration in England and Wales.[14] In Scotland, guidance was given in _Child Abuse: An Action Programme_[15] and followed by _Effective Intervention_.[16] These documents noted the importance of establishing and developing inter-agency procedures and arrangements to 'create an effective but sensitive response to child abuse'.[17]

During this period the number of reported cases of child abuse, especially child sexual abuse, showed a dramatic increase, placing increasingly complex demands on statutory and voluntary agencies. Concerns were also expressed about police investigative procedures for interviewing child victims of abuse.[18] Existing police methods, which included repetitive questioning, multiple interviews and the taking of written statements, presented difficulties for children: new police interviewing techniques were called for.

In 1988, The Home Office issued guidance to the police in England and Wales calling for a more child-centered approach in the investigation of child sexual abuse.[19] It stated that the success of police intervention should not be measured in terms of prosecution, but in terms of child protection, thus signalling a shift in police perspective. There was no similar guidance issued in Scotland.

Prior to The Home Office guidance, some police Forces had begun to review their methods of conducting child abuse investigations and their techniques for interviewing children.[20] They acknowledged the necessity of working with other agencies, particularly social work. An important development was a scheme of joint working between police and social workers known as the 'Bexley experiment'.[21] This scheme prompted other Forces and social services throughout Britain to consider similar joint arrangements. Joint working has transformed the perspective from which child protection work is carried out. The interpretation and practice of inter-agency working varies considerably, however, and a number of models are currently in operation.

More recently Waterhouse and Carnie (1990) examined the professional response to intra-familial child sexual abuse in four Scottish regions.[22] They found differences in the way in which the investigation of sexual abuse was organised in each area. There were also differences between police and social work departments concerning the definition of abuse. They found that inter-agency communication was vexed by competing professional objectives, disputes over the control and management of cases, unrealistic expectations of the powers and responsibilities of social workers and procedural inexperience by both agencies.

3.3 CONCLUSION

In recent years both the effectiveness and appropriateness of traditional methods of police investigation have been questioned. A number of well-publicised events have opened policing to scrutiny and have highlighted problems with police methods in relation to crimes of violence against women and children. Some proposals for change have had an impact in policy formulation. The report by Chambers and Millar in 1983, for example, was reflected in The Scottish Office circular to police in 1985. Similarly, recommendations made in the 1985 Women's National Commission Report on violence against women were taken up in The Home Office circular of 1986. Public opinion has also provided an impetus for change in the police response to violence against women and children. Police initiatives regarding sexual assault and child abuse have emerged after sustained criticism, especially from women themselves.

In recent years the police have assumed a larger role in child protection. Increased levels of reporting have meant that the police are investigating child abuse cases more frequently. The police role has moved beyond an emphasis on the apprehension of an offender, to incorporate a concern with the protection of the child. This has encouraged a shared understanding of child abuse issues with other child protection agencies. The impetus for joint working in this area has inevitably led to a reformulation of policies and the development of new working practices by all relevant agencies.

Footnotes

---

1   See for example, Pahl, J. (ed) (1985) Private Violence and Public Policy. Radford, J. (1987) Policing male violence - policing women, in: Hanmer, J & Maynard, M. (eds) Women, Violence and Social Control.
2   See for example, Dunhill, C. (ed) (1989) The Boys in Blue: Women's Challenge to the Police.
3   Chambers, G. & Tombs, J. (eds) (1984) The British Crime Survey (Scotland).
4   Berger, V. (1977) Man's Trial and Women's Tribulation: Rape Cases in the Courtroom. Hanmer, J., Radford, J., & Stanko, E. (eds) (1989) Women, Policing and Male Violence: International Perspectives.
5   This resulted in a private prosecution and a review of practice in prosecutorial decision-making. See Harper, R. & McWhinnie, A. (1983) The Glasgow Rape Case.
6   Chambers, G. & Millar, A. (1983) Investigating Sexual Assault.
7   Home Office Circular 25/1983 Investigation of Offences of Rape.
8   CC Circular 7/1985: Investigation of Complaints of Sexual Assault.
9   Women's National Commission (1985) Report on Violence against Women.
10   Home Office Circular 69/1986: Violence Against Women.
11   CC Circular 3/1990: Investigation of Complaints of Domestic Assault, SHHD. Home Office Circular 60/1990: Domestic Violence.
12   DHSS (1974); DHSS (1980); DHSS (1982); DHSS (1985); London Borough of Brent (1985); London Borough of Greenwich (1987).
13   Report of the Inquiry into Child Abuse in Cleveland 1987 (1988).
14   Working Together, DHSS and Welsh Office (1988).
15   SWSG Circular SW9/1988: Child Abuse: An Action Programme.
16   SWSG (1989) Effective Intervention. Child Abuse: Guidance on Co-operation in Scotland.
17   Ibid
18   Vizard, E., Bentovim, A. & Tranter, M. (1987) ;Interviewing Sexually Abused Children' Adoption and Fostering, 11, pp202-211.
19   Home Office Circular 52/1988: The Investigation of Child Sexual Abuse.
20   Metropolitan Police Working Party (1984).

21   A scheme of joint working set up between the Metropolitan Police and Social Services Department in the London Borough of Bexley.

22   Waterhouse, L. and Carnie, J. (1990) Child Sexual Abuse: The Professional Challenge. Report to SWSG.

CHAPTER 4

FORMULATION OF POLICE POLICY

This Chapter outlines the way in which Scottish Forces responded to calls for changes in the investigation of violent crime against women and children. Consideration is given to the main factors which affected the formulation of policy. The Chapter draws on material from police policy documents and interviews with senior officers.

4.1 THE ROLE OF THE CHIEF CONSTABLE

Decisions regarding Force policies and priorities are made by Chief Constables. A directive from the Chief Constable sets the agenda for policy change and subsequent action by other officers. Scraton (1982) notes that policy decisions made by Chief Constables are influenced by a range of factors, including political influence and public opinion.[1] Policy decisions can also be influenced by own perceptions of priorities and needs for policing in their Force area. Although Chief Constables have wide discretion in their interpretation and implementation of government guidelines, these are rarely ignored. The use of discretion, however, is important in determining the nature and focus of the response to guidelines in each Force. In some Forces, reaction to the 1985 guidance on the investigation of sexual assault was prompt, with directives issued shortly afterwards. Indeed, the initiative in Strathclyde pre-dated government guidelines. In other Forces, Chief Constable directives focused more on arrangements concerning the investigation of child abuse.

In most Forces, responsibility for reviewing practice, researching alternative strategies and the actual formulation of policy was delegated to senior officers, although all changes in policy require ratification from the Chief Constable. In a minority of Forces, the Chief Constable directly supervised policy changes.

4.2 APPROACHES TAKEN BY POLICY MAKERS

Where officers were delegated by Chief Constables to undertake research and make recommendations regarding the reformulation of policy, they were also mandated to put forward new strategies for policing. Interviews with these officers revealed a range of attitudes and approaches to the problems of violence against women and children.

4.2.1 Acknowledgement of the need for change

Of the twelve policy-makers interviewed, ten stated that they felt changes in police practice had been needed. These officers were of the opinion that the guidelines were appropriate and that a revised police approach to sexual assault, especially rape, was needed. Three spoke of the prevalence of sceptical or critical attitudes, particularly among older officers. One Detective Superintendent spoke of the need to stop the "nefarious practices" which were involved in the investigation of rape in his Force. Four referred to the Thames TV documentary, stating that what the programme showed had been "more or less typical" at the time the issue was addressed in their Force. Two officers spoke of needing to "re-educate older detectives" regarding violence against women.

All ten officers were keenly aware of the public criticism directed towards the police, which they had borne in mind throughout the period of research and review that pre-dated policy revisions. The provision of a "professional police response" was a concern for most officers. The remaining two officers felt that police policy and practice in the investigation of violent crimes against women and children did not require change. One of these officers expressed irritation at the "concern with victims" and felt that resources should be put into "dealing with real crime" such as "armed robbery".

4.2.2 A sceptical approach

Some of the officers who agreed that change was needed also indirectly defended a sceptical approach to some victims. Six officers referred to the seriousness of an allegation of rape or child abuse, saying that it required, as one Detective Superintendent put it, "vigilant and professional detecting." One DCI emphasised the need to ensure that officers allocated to investigate such crimes were "aware of the possibility of false allegations" and primed to deal with them.

4.2.3 Staffing concerns

One third of officers spoke of setting out with the intention of consolidating the role of women officers in sexual assault and child abuse investigations. They thought that women officers had an important supportive role to play in dealing with women reporting sexual assault and children who were the subject of child abuse investigations. The role of women officers was seen as giving support and assistance to the CID investigating officers.

4.2.4 Administrative concerns

In the area of child abuse, all officers referred to the pressure of increased workload brought about by higher levels of reporting. The strain on resources caused by the rising number of lengthy child abuse investigations was an important factor in the way policy makers approached the problem. One superintendent noted a concern to revise practice in order to alleviate some of the pressure on operational CID officers.

4.2.5 The desirability of joint working

There was a range of views concerning the feasibility and desirability of working with social workers. Some officers were resistant, whilst others wished to improve existing arrangements. One third wished to implement policies and arrangements that would complement social work practice. Several officers referred to the favourable influence that the Area Review/Child Protection Committees and regional SWDs had on their attitude and approach to child abuse investigations. For these officers, attendance at these meetings did much to raise their awareness of the complexity of child protection issues.

4.2.6 Concern with the victim

Most policy-makers acknowledged that male violence was a common denominator in crimes of violence against women and children, although the focus of new policy was to be victim rather than offender-linked. Several officers also referred to the need to combat the "cycle of abuse" whereby abused children could become abusers themselves.

4.2.7 Motivating factors

Interviews also revealed that officers' commitment and motivation for the task of devising new policing strategies was important. Motivating factors varied. Just over half of the officers said that they were motivated by a desire to improve the police response to sexual assault and child abuse. Three officers revealed a competitive spirit, illustrated by one Superintendent who noted a wish "not to be seen to be falling behind" in relation to initiatives in other Forces. Other motivating factors related to personal goals, such as a perceived opportunity for career advancement. The existence of policy-makers who were committed to the development of new and improved policies was important in setting standards. In some cases, it also influenced the way in which new initiatives were resourced.

4.3 INTERNAL REVIEWS OF EXISTING ARRANGEMENTS

An important starting point for policy-makers was an assessment of the problems with existing policy and police practice. Related to this was their perception of the extent to which police practice might be changed. Most Forces began by reviewing their existing resources; internal reviews of practice in the CID and Community Involvement Branches (CIB) were also undertaken.

4.3.1 Existing practice

In most Forces, when the first policy reviews were instigated, arrangements for the handling of sexual assault and child abuse cases entailed the provision, where possible, of a uniformed woman police officer (WPC) to take initial statements. In cases of rape, sexual assault and serious cases of child abuse a CID officer was assigned to conduct the investigation. Chambers and Millar (1983) found that the majority of rape and rape-related cases were assigned to CID officers of Constable rank, and that allocation appeared to be on the basis of the officers' current workload rather than the specific qualities of the officer in dealing with emotional or sensitive complainers.[2] They also found that a number of officers were involved in different capacities during the investigation.

One DCI related the shortcomings of police systems and procedures identified by a review conducted within his Force. This review found that delays were caused by waiting for a WPC to become available to interview the child; the interview was conducted as quickly as possible in order to allow the WPC to resume her other duties; several officers were involved in the investigation and several interviews and medical examinations of children often took place. There was general dissatisfaction regarding arrangements with SWDs, particularly regarding the length of time that social workers took to notify the police of a case of suspected abuse. These issues were also identified in other Forces.

4.4 A SHIFT IN EMPHASIS: RAPE TO CHILD ABUSE

Individual Forces began reviewing their policies and planning for change from 1983 onwards. It has already been noted that throughout the 1980s concern related to police conduct and practice in the investigation of sexual assault. From the late 1980s however, the police were faced with increasing demands for a more effective response to child abuse. Some senior officers held the view that until the late 1980s the police viewed and dealt with crimes of sexual violence against women and with child abuse in a similar way. Women and child victims were perceived to have more or less the same needs, with the same approach and range of police skills required in both types of investigation. They were also seen to present the same sorts of problems in investigative terms. As one Superintendent said,

"We always thought women and weans, they always go together".

A second Superintendent referred to the situation in the mid 1980's in this way,

"Children and child abuse were seen as adjuncts, if you like, to women and sexual assault because child abuse was not a problem then like it is now."

As child abuse became more of a public issue, there were demands for improvements in the professional response. More police resources were taken up in investigations and attention shifted from incidents of rape and sexual crimes against women to a concern with child abuse. This was mirrored by an emphasis on the protection of the child, which contrasted an earlier concern with detection of the offender.

4.5   A SPECIALIST RESPONSE

A consideration in all Forces was the feasibility of implementing a specialist response, with designated officers deployed in specialist teams. Some officers undertook detailed research and collected material on sexual assault and child abuse from a wide variety of sources.

4.5.1   Other initiatives

Specialist initiatives were already in operation in England and the United States. Representatives from several Scottish Forces undertook visits to some of the English specialist Units to assess their potential as models for Scottish Forces. Visits were made to Greater Manchester, Lancashire, Northamptonshire, Northumbria, West Yorkshire, the Metropolitan Police and St Mary's Sexual Assault Centre in Manchester.[3] A Strathclyde officer went further afield and visited law enforcement agencies in the United States to research aspects of specialist approaches to the investigation of rape and sexual assault.

4.5.2   Logistical considerations

Scottish Forces differ greatly in terms of area and population size, crime rates and staffing (see Appendix I). These factors were taken into account in deliberations regarding specialist provisions. Financial and staff resources were also of great importance. In Forces which covered a large area, geographical factors and the implications for communication and transport were also considered.

4.5.3   Alternatives to specialisation

Most officers were aware of the call for the establishment of specialist Units for the investigation of sexual assault made by Chambers and Millar (1983). There were also a number of arguments against the establishment of specialist teams. These were outlined by Blair (1985)[4] as follows:

i)   specialist Units would not fit well with established practice where rape was investigated by detectives;

ii) specialist Units would necessitate changes in established staffing and shift systems because most rapes were reported at night and weekends;

iii) the low incidence of sexual assault reports would not justify the maintenance of a Unit.

Instead, Blair argued for 'the introduction of specially selected, but geographically dispersed sex investigators.'[5] Three Scottish Forces considered alternatives to the specialist team approach. They explored the possibility of specialist officers who could, in addition to other responsibilities, be called upon to investigate sexual assault and child abuse. They also examined the possibility of nominated officers to act as consultants in particular investigations and, in relation to child abuse, officers to co-ordinate investigations and liaise with other agencies.

Seven of the eight Forces decided to set up specialist teams of officers. These teams were established at different times and in different ways. The exception was Northern Constabulary which appointed a centralised Child Abuse Co-ordinator and, along lines advocated by Blair, deployed local specialist officers throughout the Force area to deal with sexual assault and child abuse. This work was to be undertaken in addition to general duties.

4.5.4 Dual-responsibility Units

Although the general response was to establish specialist Units, they differ in a number of key respects, the most fundamental of which is their degree of specialisation.

Five Forces (Dumfries and Galloway, Grampian, Lothian and Borders, Strathclyde, Tayside) decided to build on existing arrangements of using women officers as the basis for developing a more formalised and structured specialist approach to sexual assault and child abuse cases. In Tayside, a 'Female Enquiry Section' had been in operation since 1981 and this provided the basis for further development. Units in all these Forces have a remit for the investigation of sexual assault and child abuse.

4.5.5 Child Protection Units

Central and Fife took an entirely new approach. Units were established exclusively for the investigation of child abuse. This entailed a greater degree of specialisation than the Units with dual responsibilities. In both Forces, there was considerable impetus and support for such an initiative from the corresponding regional SWDs. The Child Protection Units (CPUs) were in every sense joint police/social work ventures rather than police initiatives alone.

A review of possible options and models of working was undertaken in Central in 1987. Accounts of the work of the Bexley joint scheme had a strong influence on their approach. Whereas Bexley dealt only with sexual abuse, the intention in Central was for a Unit which investigated all forms of child abuse. A working party was established, jointly chaired by police and social work managers, and lengthy consultation took place with other agencies including local health authorities, RSSPCC, the Procurator Fiscal and Reporter to the Children's Panel.

Initially, Fife drew considerably from the Central initiative, although the model of working ultimately adopted in Fife was significantly different. A working party was also established in Fife to discuss the feasibility of joint working and it included representatives from a variety of local agencies.

4.6 CONTACT WITH OTHER AGENCIES

In all Forces, relationships with other agencies were important factors in policy formulation. Where they already existed, relationships and links were strengthened in a number of ways. For example, officers in the CIB, who had established links in the community and with voluntary organisations were consulted. Some Forces sought the views and advice of voluntary organisations, representatives from ethnic communities and women's groups. Others did not consult in this way.

It was in the area of child abuse that police acknowledged the necessity of gaining the support and expertise of staff in other agencies to improve their investigative and interviewing practices. Social workers were particularly important in this respect and senior officers in several Forces began consulting with their corresponding SWDs. In some cases this was at the instigation of the SWDs rather than the police.

Three Forces in particular - Central, Fife and Northern - conducted a thorough and extensive consultation process with SWDs and other agencies such as Procurators Fiscal, RSSPCC and police surgeons. Inter-agency contact was seen as vital from the outset. In Central and Fife, this was because of the perceived role and function of the CPUs and their objective of joint investigations. In Northern it was followed by the appointment of the Child Abuse Co-ordinator.

4.7 INTER-FORCE CONTACT

Some inter-Force visits within Scotland were undertaken, but apart from the contact between Fife and Central, these visits were carried out in an ad hoc way.

4.8 FORCE ORDERS

All new and revised policies are set down in individual Force instructions called Force Orders (FOs). These are formal documents which outline policing policy and operational procedure within each Force. Most Forces gave the research access to FOs which referred to the investigation of sexual assault and child abuse. Police policy-makers were also willing to discuss their contents. Force orders give a picture of individual Force responses to government guidelines. They also illustrate differences and similarities in priorities and practice across Forces.

4.8.1 Acknowledgement of public concern

The content and style of instructions differed between Forces. Several FOs were prefaced by an acknowledgement of public concern. For example, one set heralded the establishment of a Unit in the following way,

> 'The handling of cases of rape, incest, child sexual abuse and other non-accidental injury to children by all the caring agencies including the police, has been the subject of public scrutiny and debate for a number of years. Police methods of dealing with such cases are constantly reviewed and where appropriate improvements made......'

It is interesting to note that the police referred to themselves as one of the 'caring agencies' rather than an investigative agency. A second set of instructions, relating to a CPU, made a similar point and noted the alignment of the police with other agencies,

'There is general concern about the instances in this country of 'abused' or battered' children and it is felt that with ealier identification of the child at risk, by agencies with responsibility in this field, some cases might have been prevented. These agencies include doctors, social workers, district nurses, school teachers, health visitors and, by no means least, the police.'

4.8.2   Aims and objectives of Units

A small number of FOs gave a clear statement of the aims and objectives of the proposed Unit. They all emphasised the importance of professionalism in the handling of cases. For example,

'The value of the Unit will be the development of an expertise and professionalism in the handling of cases which require the utmost sensitivity and thoroughness.'

The aims of this CPU were stated as, 'to ensure prompt, skilled and sensitive investigation of all referrals of suspected or actual child abuse.'

4.8.3   Definitions of crimes

Most FOs included definitions of crimes and offences to be dealt with by Units. They also contained guidance to non-Unit officers on how to handle initial contact with those reporting sexual assault and/or child abuse. Several contained innovative elements. Three sets of instructions gave detailed definitions of child abuse which were not confined to a legal definition. For example:

'A widely used definition of child abuse states that a child is considered to be abused or at risk of abuse when the basic needs of the child are not being met through avoidable acts...
Types of abuse:
(a)   Physical abuse;
(b)   Sexual abuse;
(c)   Psychological or 'soft' battering;
(d)   Abandonment, neglect; and
(e)   Any combination of the above.'

4.8.4   Function of the Units

Several FOs included a statement outlining the role and function of the Units and the terms of reference, duties and responsibilities of specialist officers. Some sets of instructions explicitly stated that an important concern was the overall welfare of the victim and that help, advice and support should be given to the victim during all stages of the police investigation.

When referring to child abuse investigations, the overall tone of Force Orders suggested that officers should be as concerned with the protection of the child as they were with the apprehension of an offender. For example,

'The investigation of child abuse cases may be carried out concurrently by the police for two equal but distinct purposes. Firstly, the prosecution of an alleged offender against a child victim; and secondly, the protection and welfare of the child victim and other children usually in the same household as the alleged offender.'

Standard procedures to be followed by Unit staff in relation to medical examinations, identification parades and the care of productions were also given. There were marked differences between Forces regarding procedural instructions. For example, some stated that on no account should medical examinations of victims take place in a police station unless there was a designated interview suite. Others stated that it would be appropriate for medical examinations to be carried out in a police station. Other points of difference included procedures for record keeping.

4.8.5 Liaison with other agencies

Some FOs noted the need for Units to maintain close contact with other organisations and the rest of the Force. For example:

> 'Liaison will be established between Unit officers and the appropriate outside agencies including the Social Work Department, the Reporter to the Children's Panel, the Procurator Fiscal, the RSSPCC, Rape Crisis Centres etc., and a close working relationship will be developed at Divisional, Force and national level.'

On the other hand, FOs had little to say on interviewing techniques, follow-through after the investigation was completed and the provision of information to victims on developments in the case, helping agencies and medical checks.

4.9 FORCE ORDERS AND POLICY UPDATES

All Forces issued an initial set of instructions announcing policy changes and alerting officers to new or revised procedures. Six Forces have since issued updates to these documents. The later sets of instructions were the result of reviews which heralded a growth in the number of Units within the Force, or an expansion in Unit personnel. In Northern Constabulary, where Force Orders have not been updated since October 1989, the Force is considering the report by Lord Clyde on the Orkney inquiry before releasing new instructions. In Tayside, where Force Orders date from September 1988, a review is in progress and new Force Orders are expected.

Most current Force Orders have been recently updated. It can be noted, however, that most updates in Force Orders have been made in response to an increase in the number of specialist officers, designated facilities and Units themselves rather than to any internal assessment of new policies and procedures. More recently, however, there is evidence that changes to Force Orders are being made after wider consultation with a wider range of agencies. One example is in Lothian and Borders, where a new joint Code of Practice was issued after discussion with relevant agencies in the area. This Code forms part of an overall review of inter-agency guidelines for the investigation of child abuse undertaken by the Child Protection Committees of both Lothian and Borders Regional Councils, on which Lothian and Borders Police are represented. The views of victims have yet to be included in changes to Force Orders and it can be noted that successful policy change is not achieved simply by the adoption of new policy, but by a continual process of review and assessment. The importance of a regular review of policy and procedure in relation to crimes of violence against women and children should not be overlooked. The wealth of current research in both areas offers new findings and perspectives. The updating of all Force Orders could take more account of this.

4.10 CONCLUSION

An early finding of this research was the wide variation between Forces in relation to the development and implementation of new policy for the investigation of sexual assault and child abuse. The establishment of specialist Units represents a more unified response to these crimes in Scotland, but there is no common policy for the Units.

A range of factors influenced the development of policy in each Force. These included staffing, Force area and population size. Other factors were Force-specific. They included: attitudes to and perceptions of the problem of sexual assault and child abuse by policy-makers, the level of reporting of these crimes, existing operational procedures and investigative arrangements, existing professional relationships between the police and other agencies, established working relationships between individuals in these agencies, links with voluntary organisations and the level of commitment and motivation of individual senior officers.

It can be seen that Scottish police Forces responded at different times and in different ways to calls for change. The remit and focus of individual Units reflected the interplay of these demands and the way in which priorities in each Force were established.

Footnotes

1   Scraton, P. (1985) The State of the Police.
2   Chambers, G. and Millar, A. (1983).
3   St Mary's Sexual Assault Referral Centre was opened within St Mary's Hospital, Manchester in 1987, and is a joint initiative between Greater Manchester Police and South Manchester Area Health Authority. The Centre has WPCs taking statements, full-time nurse counsellors and female police surgeons on call
4   Blair, I. (1985) Investigating Rape: A New Approach for Police, pp75-78.
5   Ibid. p77.

CHAPTER 5

THE STRUCTURE OF UNITS AND DEPLOYMENT OF SPECIALIST OFFICERS

The organisational structure of the specialist Units has implications for the way in which their work is carried out. This Chapter outlines the basic structure devised for the Units in each Force. It examines staffing policies and describes the systems of management and internal administrative arrangements which were established.

5.1 STAFFING THE UNITS

An important consideration for senior officers charged with the task of setting up the Units was the selection of staff to work in them. Police policy-makers acknowledged from the early stages that the success of the Units would be dependent on the attitude and approach of the Unit officers. Staff selection and training were therefore crucial factors.

A sensitive response to crimes of violence against women and children poses a number of challenges for the police. It involves a range of social and investigative skills and the need for a sympathetic, understanding and patient approach by individual police officers.[1] This view was endorsed by the SHHD guidelines to the police on the investigation of sexual assault. They noted the need for officers who would have the necessary skills to conduct the investigation 'with tact, understanding and full regard to [the woman's] well-being.'[2] Forces differed in their approach to the selection of personnel to become specialist officers. There were differences not only in terms of selection criteria, but also in the manner of appointment. There were, however, a number of concerns regarding the choice of the right officers for the job. One was that officers would have "the right approach". Senior officers suggested that Unit officers would be "patient, gentle and prepared to offer sympathy", and would be "understanding". A second concern was that officers would be "good investigators", that they would be "meticulous" and they would be "good at getting the facts." A third concern was that officers would have built up police experience. They would be officers who "were not too young in service", who had "at least 3-4 years length of service" who had "background experience of general police work that would have brought them into contact with the public" and who had "some experience in these kinds of cases." Some Forces devised job descriptions for staff in the Units, but these were for Sergeants or Detective Sergeants rather than for Constables or Detective Constables.

In five Forces specialist officers are exclusively female (Dumfries and Galloway, Lothian and Borders, Tayside, Strathclyde, Northern). In three Forces it was decided to build on existing arrangements where women uniformed officers assisted in investigations. Selection of suitable candidates to become specialist officers was straightforward. Policewomen who had most frequently and, in the opinion of Divisional Commanders, most ably undertaken the work in the past were selected, providing they had at least three years general police service. In three of these Forces, it is now compulsory for all women officers to undergo specialist training so that they can be seconded to the Units at some stage.

In the remaining three Forces, the gender of specialist officers was a point for discussion. In Central and Fife a decision was taken to ensure that there would be a gender mix of officers in the CPUs. Policy-makers in both Forces said that they thought the work of the CPUs could be seen as low priority if they were staffed only by female officers. Another reason was that the CPUs would be staffed by social workers of both sexes, and policy makers in both agencies were keen for police to match these staffing arrangements. When the first Unit was established in Grampian, it had an all-female staff. Six months later a male DS was appointed as a deliberate strategy to enhance the status of the Unit. A second change came about some months later with the replacement of a female DC with a male DC.

5.1.1 Appointment procedure

Within the police, officers are moved between police stations and branches of the police in order to gain wide experience. Young uniformed officers are given little or no choice regarding a change of job within the Force and are simply informed where and what their next job will be. With the exception of the two CPUs, all Forces adopted this general procedure when appointing officers to the Units. The amount of notice given to individual officers about secondment to the Units varied from several weeks to two days. Since the establishment of the Units, particularly in Forces where it is mandatory for all post-probation female uniformed officers to undergo training in the investigation of sexual assault and child abuse, policewomen know that there is a strong chance that they will be moved to a Unit.

A recent development in Lothian and Borders and some Divisions of Strathclyde is the 'aide' system, whereby young female officers are temporarily assigned a Unit for a limited period prior to secondment. The aim of the system is to familiarise officers with the work of the Unit and also to asses their suitability for the work.

Central and Fife advertised internally for volunteers to work in the Units. Both Forces had a low response rate and eventually suitable individuals were approached directly for the work. Later, adverts to replace existing staff brought a relatively large number of applicants. These were carefully screened by senior officers to ascertain if officers were applying because of the favourable working hours kept by the Units (see 5.2.4).

5.2 INTERNAL ORGANISATION OF UNITS

In all Forces except Strathclyde and Northern, officers are organised in a single team or teams of officers of Constable or Detective Constable rank, supervised by a promoted officer of the rank of Sergeant or Detective Sergeant. Table 5.1 shows the numbers of officers in each Unit and their allocation. In Forces where there is more than one Unit, the organisational structure is of a main Unit (usually based in police headquarters) forming a centralised administrative base to oversee the work of 'satellite' Units situated in other territorial Divisions. The 'satellites' retain a degree of autonomy in that daily supervision falls under the Divisional Commander or CID officer. The exception to this is Strathclyde where there is one Unit based in each of the fifteen territorial Divisions. Each Unit is autonomous and its work is overseen by the Divisional DCI. Because of its large Force area and dispersed rural population, Northern operates a system whereby individual officers from the uniformed branch or CIB undertake investigations and assist CID in cases of sexual assault and child abuse. The Child Abuse Co-ordinator, who holds the rank of Sergeant, provides a centralised point for the supervision of child abuse cases.

Table 5.1 Number and location of Scottish police specialist Units (September 1992)

Force	Date of Inception	Resources
Central Child Protection Unit	Jan 1989	1 centralised unit with a Force-wide remit. Administrative office located in police station and staffed by 5 officers (1 male DS and 4DCs). Accountable to CID. Joint investigations of child abuse undertaken with 9 designated social workers based in 5 social work area offices. Use of 3 'interview suites' with shower and medical examination facilities located in police HQ and 2 sub-Div HQs. Video recording and play back facilities.
Fife Child Protection Unit	May 1990 - Jul 1992	1 unit serving one police Division. Located in converted house and staffed by 3 officers (1 female Sgt, 1 male DC and 1 female CONs) and 4 social workers (1 female senior social worker and 3 social workers, 2 female and 1 male) and a clerical support worker. Interview room on premises, no shower or medical examination facilities. Second Unit covering remaining Force Area. Staffed by 4 officers (1 male DS and 3 female CONs) and 4 social work staff (1 male senior and 3 social workers (2 female and 1 male). Interview room on premises, no shower or medical examination facilities.
Dumfries and Galloway Female and Child Unit	Jun 1991	1 centralised unit with a Force-wide remit. Administrative officer located in Police HQ and staffed by 3 female officers (1DS and 2DCs). Accountable to CID. Plans underway for interview suite with shower and medical facilities to be built in new HQ building (due for completion 1993).
Grampian Female Enquiry Section Renamed 1992 Female and Child Enquiry Section	Jun 1989 - Aug 1989 - Oct 1990	1 main unit in Police HQ overseen by DI and staffed by 6 officers (3 DSs, 2 male and 1 female and 3 DCs, 2 female and 2 male). Accountable to CID. Main administrative base with remit for City district. Interview suite with shower and medical examination facilities. 'Satellite' unit staffed by 2 female DCs at sub-Div HQ with remit for that Division. No interview or medical examination facilities. 'Satellite' unit staffed by 2 female DCs at Sub-Div HQ with remit for that Division. No interview or medical examination facilities.

Table 5.1 (continued)

Force	Date of Inception	Resources
Lothian and Borders Woman and Child Unit	Feb 1988 - Feb 1988 - Apr 1990 - Apr 1990	1 main unit in Div HQ, staffed by 5 female officers (1DS and 4DCs). Administrative base with remit for City district (4 Divisions). Interview suite with shower facilities on-site and at a second location. No medical examination facilities. 'Satellite' unit staffed by 2 female DCs at Div HQ with remit for that Division. Interview and shower facilities on-site. 'Satellite' unit staffed by 2 female DCs at Div HQ with remit for that Division. Interview and shower facilities on-site. 'Satellite' unit staffed by 2 female DCs at Div HQ with remit for that Division. Interview and shower facilities onsite and at 3 other locations throughout Divisional area.
Strathclyde Female and Child Unit	July 1984	15 units at Div HQ of each of the 15 Divisions of the Force. Each unit is staffed by 4 female CONs with exception of one unit which is staffed by 3 female CONs. Each unit run on a localised basis and overseen by the Divisional DCI and accountable to CID. There are 8 'interview suites' with shower and medical facilities located in 6 Divisional HQs. 2 or 3 Units in adjacent divisions share the use of interview suites.
Tayside Child and Female Specialist Enquiry Section	Sept 1988	Main unit in Police HQ staffed by 5 female officers (1 SGT and 4 CONs). Administrative base with remit for City district. Overseen by Inspector and accountable to Superintendent, CIB. On-site interview suite with showers and medical examination facilities due for completion Dec 1992. 2 CAFSES Constables located at Div HQ (Eastern Division) with a remit for that Division. No interview facilities. 2 CAFSES Constables located at Div HQ (Western Division) with a remit for that Division. No interview facilities.
Northern Child Abuse Co-ordinator and Specialist Officers	Oct 1989	Child Abuse Co-ordinator (female SGT) based in Police administrative offices in Inverness with remit for coordinating all child abuse enquiries and joint police/social work investigations Force-wide. Also responsible for overseeing female officers (CONs) investigating sexual assault and child abuse located at police stations across Force area. Accountable to CID and Community Involvement. Interview suite with shower, medical examination and video recording facilities located in extensively converted house away from police premises.

Source: Force documents and interviews with senior officers and Unit officers.

5.2.1 Accountability of the Units

Units differ in terms of which branch of the Police they are located in and this dictates their internal command structure and line of accountability.

In six out of the eight Forces, the Units were formed as part of the CID, which has responsibility for the investigation of serious crime. Although the size of the CID and the complexity of its command structure varies between Forces, it can generally be said that a DCI based at Divisional Headquarters has overall responsibility for all CID operations within that Division (including the Units). A Detective Superintendent or a Detective Chief Superintendent supervises all CID operations in a group of Divisions.

CAFSES, in Tayside Police, is part of the CIB, the branch responsible for community policing. Overall supervision of CAFSES is by a CIB Superintendent via a Chief Inspector.

In Northern Constabulary, the specialist officers deployed throughout the Force consult with the Child Abuse Co-ordinator, but are operationally responsible to Divisional DCIs, and through them to a Detective Superintendent. The Child Abuse Co-ordinator is responsible on an operational basis to a Detective Superintendent (CID) and responsible on a day-to-day administrative basis to the Officer-in Charge, CIB.

5.2.2 Secondment to the Units

Officers are seconded to work in the Units for a fixed period. Most Forces set this at three years when Units were first incepted, although recently the trend has been for a secondment of two to two and a half years . Several officers reported being told that they would be seconded for a specified period, but have remained in the Unit for longer than they orginally understood.

In some Forces, working in the Units is unpopular. There are different views as to whether officers are able to leave the Units if they dislike or find the work difficult. Many senior officers said it would be possible for officers to leave at any stage but Unit officers disagreed, pointing out that it simply is "not done" to attempt to get a transfer out of any job in the police, not least from the Units.

5.2.3 Designated status of Unit officers

Although most Units are formed as part of the operational arm of the CID, the majority of specialist officers are recruited from the uniform branch, and some from the CIB. There are very few women detective officers. Of the eighteen Unit officers interviewed, only four had previous detective experience.

In four Forces (Grampian, Lothian and Borders, Central, Dumfries and Galloway) where the Unit was formed as part of the CID, all Unit officers are designated CID officers, whether or not they were detective officers prior to secondment to the Unit. During their secondment period they are given the title of Detective Constables, wear plain clothes and receive a CID allowance. At the end of the secondment period, Unit officers revert to uniformed officer status.

Although Unit officers assume the rank of Detective and the Units are part of the CID, they are not seen as "real CID" because they have not undergone CID training which includes input on how to conduct suspect interviews.

Several Unit officers thought that the detective status which accompanied becoming a Unit officer caused some animosity from Divisional CID officers who had to pass examinations, undergo training and make special application to become CID officers. For this reason, a decision was taken in Fife Constabulary that Unit officers who were not already CID would not receive Detective status for the duration of their secondment. In Tayside, officers are drawn from the CIB and uniformed branches and are designated CIB officers for the length of their secondment. In Strathclyde, all officers are drawn from the uniformed branch and, although the Units are attached to the CID, the officers do not receive CID status for the duration of their secondment. In Central, officers are drawn from both the uniformed branch and the CID and they are assessed for suitability after attending a joint police/social work training course.

All specialist officers are plain-clothed. Exceptions to this may be occasions in Northern where the specialist officer is called away from her uniformed duties to attend a sexual assault or child abuse case.

5.2.4 Hours of working

Units differ in their working hours. A two shift system is worked in all Units except in Fife and Dumfries and Galloway, where they are staffed between 9 am and 5 pm.

Table 5.2 Working hours of Units

Force	Coverage
Central CPU	09.00 - 22.00 Mon - Fri 09.00 - 17.00 Sat Call out system after hours
Fife CPU	09.00 - 17.00 Mon - Fri Call out system after hours
Dumfries & Galloway	09.00 - 17.00 Mon - Sun Call out system after hours
Grampian	08.00 - 22.00 Mon - Sun Call out system after hours
Lothian & Borders	09.00 - 22.00 Mon - Sun Call out system after hours
Strathclyde	08.00 - 23.00 Mon - Sun 23.00 - 7.00 Night-shift One Unit officer will cover 3 Divisions on nightshift. Each officer works 4 night shift weeks per year.
Tayside	08.00 - 23.00 Mon - Sat Call out system after hours

In Northern Constabulary, specialist officers work the same shift system which is in operation in the station/Division where they are based. A call out system operates if there is no specialist officer on duty. In Strathclyde, there is often only one specialist officer on duty per shift. This can place severe limits on the availibility of a specialist response.

Some Forces operate a system where there is an hour overlap between shifts (eg. 8 am - 4 pm and 3 pm - 11 pm). Overlapping shifts mean that officers have an opportunity to hand over or discuss work with another Unit officer. Where this does not exist, problems can arise in terms of continuity and/or organisation of work.

The police shift system does not always correspond with the hours worked by social workers and this can cause problems in terms of joint working. Most child abuse referrals come to police attention during the week, when SWDs and schools are open and officers tend not to receive such cases at the weekend. Several officers indicated that it is often most convenient to interview witnesses at weekends and in the evening, particularly in child abuse cases. Interviewing at these times, they felt, causes least inconvenience to the witnesses concerned who may otherwise have to take time from work or school. Social workers are not always available at these times.

In Strathclyde, only one specialist officer is on night duty to cover three or four adjacent Divisions. In a highly populated area like Glasgow city centre, this means that the officer may not be able to respond to all calls. Neither does it ensure that the same officer will continue with the case throughout the investigation, as the case will be picked up the following day by the specialist officer from the Division in which it originated.

5.3   DEDICATED FACILITIES

The provision of dedicated facilities for the interviewing of victims was strongly recommended in the Home Office guidance to police in England and Wales; there were no such recommendations made in the SHHD guidance to Scottish Forces. There was, however, a recommendation that medical examination of victims of sexual assault should take place in a

'proper clinical environment so as to reduce stress and produce an atmosphere of care and concern.'[3]

Most Forces have dedicated facilities for the interviewing of victims of child abuse and sexual assault. Those who do not, have plans to build special interview suites. Table 5.1 shows the Units which are equipped with such facilities.

Interview suites are similar in lay-out and facilities. They usually consist of a suite of rooms comprising one or two interviewing rooms, a medical examination room and an adjoining shower room with a wash-hand basin and toilet. The interview room is usually decorated in pastel colours (pinks, greys and greens are common) and is furnished with soft carpeting, a couch, several easy chairs and coffee table. There are prints on the walls, pot plants, lamps and women's magazines, tea and coffee making facilities, ashtrays and often a telephone. Some suites have a separate room for interviewing children. This is similar in layout with children's toys, books and pictures, beanbags, a television and selection of children's videos. Some interview rooms have facilities for the video-recording of children's evidence.

Not all suites incorporate medical examination rooms, but those that do resemble a GP's surgery without the clutter of books and files. These rooms are for the sole use of victims of sexual assault and child abuse. There is a desk and chairs, telephone, sink, examination table with magnifying lamp and usually a screen. Medical examination rooms are equipped with what are known as 'Rape Kits' - individual cellophane wrapped kits containing swabs, sample bottles and containers for the collection of blood, semen and other specimens and labels and forms to be filled in by the examining doctor and attendant Unit officer.

A shower room with hand basin, bidet and toilet usually adjoins the medical room. These rooms contain a full range of toiletries - soap, shampoo, talcum powder, sanitary napkins and tampons - as well as towels, hairdryers and a selection of terry cloth gowns in sizes appropriate for childrens and adults. Nappies are also usually stocked. The rooms in the suite are lockable from inside and outside and keys are usually held by the Unit officers, who are located in office-accommodation adjacent to or close to the interview suites.

With the exception of Northern Constabulary, where interview facilities are located in a converted suburban police house, and Fife where police and social workers are located together on premises for the sole use of the CPU team, all interview suites are located on police premises. Some have separate entrances from the main police station, enabling entry without having to walk past the main desk. Others can only be reached by walking through police offices. Not all are on the ground floor. One suite has a particularly unfortunate location next to the police recreation room. Several suites are located close to general CID accommodation which, although convenient for liaison between the Unit and CID officers, can mean there is a lot of noise and activity nearby.

5.3.1 Access to vehicles

Specialist officers may have to travel in order to reach complainers, they may have to transport complainers, interview witnesses and undertake follow-up interviews. In child abuse investigations, officers may have to meet up with social workers throughout the Force or Divisional area. In several Forces, distances may be great so transportation is important. Access to vehicles in the Units differs significantly across Forces. For example, in Central CPU there are two new vehicles allocated for the sole use of the CPU officers. Fife CPU, Dumfries and Galloway and one Unit in Strathclyde all have one car allocated to them. There are no cars allocated in the remaining Forces and Unit officers have to rely on the availibility of CID or CIB cars. According to Unit officers this is a highly unsatisfactory arrangement and is often an impediment to their work. Several Unit officers spoke of having to "hitch hike" across Divisional areas, getting lifts in police cars from one station to another. Unit officers also spoke of being unable to clear their desks of small or routine tasks without the use of a car. As one Unit officer pointed out,

> "If we had a vehicle, I could go out on a Saturday and finish a number of wee jobs quickly, such as chasing up witnesses and finishing witness statements and that. Instead these jobs sit on my desk for ages and I can never clear them." (Officer 6)

5.4 ADVERTISING THE UNITS

When each Unit was opened, press releases were sent to local newspapers and articles were published to announce the opening of the Unit, giving brief details about the work of the specialist officers. All Units have given talks and presentations about their work to other agencies and community groups, schools, nurses, GPs, church groups, Childrens Panel members, RSSPCC, Victim Support Schemes and some women's groups. Some Units have distributed information about their work in the form of leaflets to doctors' surgeries and medical clinics, although this does not appear to have been done on any systematic basis.

It is interesting to note that the telephone numbers of the Units are not listed in any local telephone directories, although all police stations and many other specialist branches of the police are listed, including the Dog Branch, Drugs Branch and Fraud Squad. This does not make it easy for members of the public to contact the Units. A full list of specialist Units is given in Appendix 2.

5.5 AWARENESS BY OTHER OFFICERS

The majority of Unit officers felt that, apart from the CID and the CIB, little is known about the existence of the Units by other police officers. Even where officers are aware of the Unit, their knowledge of the nature and the amount of work undertaken by Unit officers is limited.

In some Forces, the Units are known by a number of derogatory names, including 'The Fanny Squad', 'The Nappy Squad' and 'The Women and Weans Group'. As one Unit officer pointed out, "they think we sit here all day drinking tea and knitting." Another said that whenever she leaves the building, other officers accuse her of going shopping.

Virtually all child abuse cases are notified to the police via the SWD or schools. Notification does not follow the usual police channels by means of an emergency call or over the police radio system. It is usually made by means of a direct telephone call to the Unit from the agency concerned, and this does not initially register in the control or radio room. General police awareness of the work of the Units is thus restricted.

Unit officers have devised various methods of advertising their work to the rest of the Force. These include making sure that their involvement in investigations and referrals are noted on the daily information report which records items of interest, arrests and crimes that have occurred in the preceding twenty-four hours. They also make crime reports, regardless of whether the crime is detected. As Officer 5 pointed out,

> "because an offender is not found, that does not mean that the crime has not happened, and we have not spent a lot of time working on it."

In an attempt to ascertain how much information is known about the Units by other officers and how easy it is for members of the public to contact them, telephone calls were made to twenty police stations and Divisional headquarters across Scotland asking for the local Unit. In six cases the researcher was put through to the Unit, or given its telephone number. In five cases, the researcher was asked to call police headquarters for the information. In three cases the researcher was asked to call back, during which time the site and the telephone number of the Unit was located. In another three cases the number of three other police stations was given. In one case, the researcher was referred to a social work area office and in the remaining two cases, the researcher was told to contact the CID in police headquarters.

5.6 CONCLUSION

The organisational structure of each specialist Unit has implications for the way in which its work is carried out. Different arrangements exist between Forces in the way that Units are staffed and managed. There are several advantages to having promoted officers working within the Units. Firstly, the presence of a promoted officer enhances the status of the Unit. Secondly, it is seen by many Unit officers as an indication that the work is sufficiently important to warrant having a promoted officer. It also indicates the possibility for promotion within the Unit. Thirdly, the Unit is cohesive and self-contained with a Detective Sergeant or Sergeant directly supervising work and offering consultation and advice. Fourthly, the Unit has identity and autonomy and is not seen merely as an adjunct to a particular branch of the police. Fifthly, there is a more even distribution of workload. Responsibility for the allocation of cases lies with a Detective Sergeant or Sergeant, who has knowledge of each officer's current workload. Finally, in terms of management, Unit officers feel that they have someone to "fight their corner" and provide a direct channel through which they can make requests or discuss problems.

Length of secondment varies between Forces and Units have not yet settled on an agreed period of secondment. With few exceptions, officers are given little choice on secondment to the Units. In some Forces, the work of the Units is viewed with some derision by other officers, an issue which is discussed more fully in Chapter 12. There appears to be no method of 'opting out' should officers find the work difficult or unpleasant. This raises the question of whether officers who do not want to undertake such work should be asked to do so. It also has implications for the quality of service offered in the Units.

Most Units are accountable to the CID. The designation of Unit officers as CID presents problems for specialist officers in some Forces.

The lines of accountability for Units differ between Forces. There appear to be advantages in the model of a centralised Unit acting as an administrative base where there is more than one Unit.

The shift system in some Forces means that there is no overlap between them. In some cases, only one officer is on duty per shift. The drawbacks to such an arrangement are discussed in Chapters 9 and 11. The different hours worked by police and social workers can inconvenience joint arrangements in child abuse investigations. An exception to this is the Fife CPU where police and social workers work together in the Unit. Organisational issues affecting arrangements between the Units and social workers are discussed more fully in Chapter 11. Lack of vehicles can also impede the work of the Units.

Finally it can be difficult to make direct contact with the Units. More systematic and imaginative methods of making the Units more accessible to those reporting sexual assault and child abuse are needed.

Footnotes

---

1   Chambers, G and Millar, A. (1983); Waterhouse , L. and Carnie, J. (1990); Vizard et al (1987)
2   CC Circular 7/1985
3   Ibid.

CHAPTER 6

WOMEN OFFICERS AND THE INVESTIGATION OF SEXUAL ASSAULT
AND CHILD ABUSE

The majority of specialist officers are women. This Chapter considers the effects of deploying women officers in this way and its implications for the policing of crimes of violence against women and children.

6.1 POLICE WOMEN'S DEPARTMENTS

Prior to the 1975 Sex Discrimination Act, women police officers were deployed under different organisational arrangements to male officers.[1] Women officers were organised into separate 'police women's departments' which undertook specific functions such as dealing with female victims and offenders, children, juveniles and missing persons. This meant that female officers were more experienced in this work than their male colleagues. One consequence of the 1975 Act was that police women's departments were to be integrated into the mainstream of policing. Women officers were recruited on the same basis as men, they were assigned to the same duties and were eligible for promotion and transfer to other departments on the same basis as male officers.[2]

There was some resistance to integration by senior officers throughout Britain. One concern was that the abolition of the separate police women's departments would result in a loss of the skill and expertise which female officers had built up in certain areas of policing, particularly in relation to women and children. In 1979, the Report of the Edmund-Davies Inquiry on the Police noted with concern the 'loss in relation to what might be called the social service role of women police officers resulting from the assimilation of women officers into general police work.[3]

6.2 WOMEN'S WORK

The argument that expertise might be lost once women officers were integrated into mainstream policing was based on an assumption that such 'social service' work was not part of 'real' policing. Thus, when women officers became 'real' police officers they would not continue their social service work.

Integration also meant that male officers would be expected to undertake work which was previously done by women. Since the 1975 Act, however, women officers have, in addition to their other general duties, continued to be involved in tasks that were once part of the remit of the police women's departments. This is less so for male officers, supporting the idea that the work can only be done by women officers.

Commentators have pointed to the fact that, within the police, work dealing with women and children is held to be 'women's work'.[4] Within police occupational culture, women's work incorporates the more conspicuous social welfare aspects of policing. Women's work requires little physical strength, needs a 'gentle touch', and a 'caring approach'. Interviews with senior officers confirmed this view. When referring to the qualities required by officers to undertake work in the Units, several senior officers referred to women officers being more "supportive", "patient" and "more attuned" to the work than their male counterparts. Furthermore, the role of the specialist officer is explicitly stated as one of care and support, a role that women officers are "best at", according to several senior officers interviewed.

'Social welfare' work is generally avoided by male officers.[5] In police culture, it has been pointed out, this is inextricably bound up with a masculinist view of male and female roles.[6] The police epitomise what Smith and

Gray (1983) referred to as a 'cult of masculinity',[7] which places importance on male values of toughness and strength, whereby women are effectively marginalised. Despite moves towards integration, attitudes towards policewomen remain entrenched. Research into the general attitudes of police officers towards women in the Force has shown that they are accepted only as much as they do 'womens work'.[8]

Chambers and Millar (1983) documented the unpopularity for male detectives of dealing with sexual assault cases. The study also pointed to the difficulty that male officers encountered in eliciting statements from female complainers and their general reluctance to use WPCs who had little experience in taking statements. Sexual assault cases are unpopular with detectives for other reasons, in particular because they do little for what Young (1991) termed 'the essential CID cause of returning a good conviction rate.'[9] There is also an exceptionally high acquittal rate in sexual offence trials, which a recent Scottish study showed to be as high as 78% in rape trials.[10]

Working with children is also seen as 'women's work.' Interviews with senior police and Unit officers confirmed that officers undertaking child abuse investigations are commonly viewed by other officers as 'glorified social workers'. Such work is seen as 'soft policing', rather than 'real' police work. It is generally unpopular with non-Unit officers until, as pointed out to the researchers a number of times, they understand the nature of the work or they lose their fear of investigating such cases. Closer working relationships with social workers appears to have reinforced this view of the work as 'soft' policing.

Furthermore, child abuse investigations can be very time-consuming, entailing interviews not only with the child, but also with the child's siblings and other family members, friends, neighbours and teachers. The work is routine and often tedious. By allocating such work to specialist officers, it eases the workload of the CID.

6.3   THE GENDER OF SPECIALIST OFFICERS

The Edmund-Davies Report put forward the recommendation that,

> 'consideration should be given to the establishment of specialist departments staffed by suitable women <u>and</u> men.'[11]

These departments would undertake the range of work previously handled by women officers alone. The intention here was to integrate police officers of both genders into work which involved women and children.

Similarly, Chambers and Millar (1983) identified a number of reasons why specialist officers dealing with sex crime investigations should not be exclusively female. One reason was a danger that women officers dealing exclusively with such cases would become detached from general police work and feel that they had a less important role than their male colleagues. A second reason was

> 'that properly trained male officers <u>should</u> be more involved in the types of duties that a specialised Unit would perform. There is otherwise a danger that such work would be regarded as of a low priority if only women were involved.'[12]

When referring to the selection of suitable officers for work in the investigation of sexual assault, the SHHD guidelines to police picked up this theme by stating,

'Sympathy in the interviewing officer is more important than his or her sex, but it is important that experienced female interviewing officers are available; and complainers should always be asked whether they wish to see a female officer.' [13]

Despite these considerations, specialist officers in five Forces (Lothian and Borders,Dumfries and Galloway, Northern, Strathclyde, and Tayside) are exclusively female and there is no indication that this gender balance will change in the immediate future.

6.4 WOMEN IN SCOTTISH FORCES

Chambers and Millar (1983) noted that, despite the 1975 Act, the percentage of women officers in two Scottish Forces had not risen as much as in English Forces, where numbers of women officers doubled between 1974 and 1981. In 1981 the percentage of women officers in Lothian and Borders and Strathclyde Police were 6.5% and 5.2% respectively.[14] As Table 6.1 shows, the numbers in both Forces have shown only a slight increase and women officers are not well represented in Scottish Police overall.

Table 6.1   Women officers in Scottish Police Forces (December 1991)

Force	% of women officers
Central	10.0
Dumfries and Galloway	11.0
Fife	10.3
Grampian	13.0
Lothian and Borders	10.6
Northern	9.3
Strathclyde	8.6
Tayside	9.8
Total (all Forces)	9.2

Source : Report by HM Chief Inspector of Constabulary for Scotland (1991).

Female officers interviewed for the research referred to a lack of promotion opportunities. Other research has indicated an imbalance in promotion opportunities for women in the police.[15] As Table 6.2 shows, there were few policewomen in senior positions and none above the rank of Superintendent in Scottish Forces at the end of 1991.

Table 6.2   Rank held by women officers in Scottish Police Forces (December 1991)

Rank	Total no	No of women	% of women
Superintendent	145	2	1.3
Chief Inspector	254	4	1.5
Inspector	712	14	1.9
Sergeant	2,048	65	3.1
Constable	10,660	1,272	11.9

Source : Report by HM Chief Inspector of Constabulary for Scotland (1991).

Chambers and Millar (1983) also pointed to the paucity of women detectives, and noted that if specialist officers were to be recruited from the CID, this would necessitate large increases in female CID staffing levels.[16] The number of female detectives has not increased significantly in the ten years since the study, and at least two Scottish Forces have no female CID officers at all.

6.5 CONCLUSION

In many ways, the nature of the work undertaken by specialist officers in the Units resembles that done by women officers in the old police women's departments. The majority of specialist officers are women and in some Forces specialist training and secondment to a Unit is mandatory for all women officers. Because of this there is a concern that the Units may be a retrospective step for women officers to the situation which existed in the police before the Sex Discrimination Act.

Following integration, the police were faced with assimilating women into mainstream policing. In some Forces the Units provided an expedient means of mobilising women officers into areas of policing for which they were perceived to be better suited than male officers. Women officers in the Units are deployed in marginal areas of policing, away from 'real policing' which is represented by mainstream detective work. Their role is one of providing care for victims and supporting the CID. Assisting the CID by undertaking aspects of the investigation which are troublesome, time-consuming and sometimes tedious, they relieve some of the workload of detective officers.

Because the Units are relatively new, it is not yet possible to say whether they represent one promotion possibility for women officers. Alternatively, they may represent a ghetto for female officers, whether they are promoted or not. Much of the work undertaken by specialist officers is seen as 'women's work' and for that reason it can be marginalised and viewed as low status work by other officers. There are also implications here for the way that violence against women and children is viewed as marginal within police culture. At the same time, however, the Units are a positive manifestation of the new approach by police to sexual assault and child abuse, satisfying the public's call for something to be done about violence against women and children.

Footnotes

1   Chambers, G. and Millar, A. (1983) p 114.
2   Jones, S. (1986) Policewomen and Equality: Formal Policy V Informal Practice.
3   Committee of Inquiry on the Police, Report III (1979) p88.
4   See for example, Chambers, G. and Millar, A. (1983); Jones, S. (1986): Young, M. (1991) An Inside Job: Policing and Police Culture in Britain.
5   Young, M. (1991).
6   Ibid.; Jones (1986); Chambers, G. and Millar, A. (1983); Edwards (1989).
7   Smith, D. and Gray, J (1983) Police and People in London.
8   Ibid.; Young, M. (1991); Edwards, S (1989).
9   Young, M. (1991).
10   Brown, B., Burman, M., and Jamieson, L. (1992) Sexual History and Sexual Character Evidence in Sexual Offence Trials.
11   Committee of Inquiry on the Police (1979) p88.
12   Chambers, G. and Millar, A. (1983) p132.
13   CC Circular 7/1985.
14   Chambers, G. and Millar, A. (1983) p115.
15   Jones, S. (1986).
16   Chambers, G. and Millar, A. (1983) p132.

CHAPTER 7

TRAINING FOR SPECIALIST OFFICERS

This Chapter documents the development of training for specialist officers in each Force and summarises the range of current training provision. It also gives officers' views on the training they received.

7.1 BASIC POLICE TRAINING

During their two year probationary period, all Scottish police recruits undergo basic training which includes input on rape and sexual assault. Information on the relevant law and procedure is presented, usually by senior officers. There may be input from outside speakers such as Procurators Fiscal, police surgeons and forensic scientists. In recent years, most Forces have modified basic training to include more information on child abuse, with additional input by regional SWDs.

Post-probation, formal training is more discretionary and is dependent on factors such as overall training provisions within each Force, length of service, promotion or placement in a specific branch or specialism. Detective training, for example, includes information on the law, police procedure and medical and forensic evidence in relation to sexual offences against adults and children.

Prior to the establishment of the Units, additional training for the investigation of child abuse and sexual assault was patchy or non-existent. Where such training did exist, it focused solely on the law relating to rape and other sexual offences and the taking of comprehensive statements from complainers. No male officers attended these courses which, on the whole, contained little reference to child abuse or the interviewing of children.

7.2 CALLS FOR SPECIALIST TRAINING

Chambers and Millar (1983) called for a thorough revision of police training for uniformed and CID officers on the investigation of rape and rape-related offences. They recommended a form of training that would focus on interviewing skills and include material to provide an insight into the reality of sexual violence for women.[1] The SHHD guidelines which followed the publication of this study urged Chief Constables to review their Force training policies concerning the investigation of sexual assault.[2]

From the mid-1980s, Forces with training courses for WPCs began to revise and extend them. New courses were introduced in some Forces which had no such arrangements. These early courses had limited or no input on the law and procedures relating to child abuse. It was not until the late 1980s that Scottish Forces began to turn their attention to more detailed training for child abuse, following government guidance which called on regional authorities to review their investigative procedures and to develop inter-agency training.[3]

7.3 CURRENT TRAINING FOR SPECIALIST OFFICERS

All Forces now have some form of training strategy for specialist officers. There is, however, no national training standard or curriculum for specialist officers and there is significant variation between Forces in the structure, content, timing and quality of the training. Force policy and priorities, training resources, support from senior officers and links with other agencies are all important factors.

Seven of the specialist officers interviewed in this study had undergone training which pre-dated their secondment to the Unit, often by a substantial period of time (three years in three cases). In each of these cases, they felt that the time lapse was too great. Of the seven officers who had received training after their secondment to a Unit, one had been in the post for two and a half years and another for one year. Both felt they would have benefited from some training at an earlier stage. Most officers felt that the optimum point to undergo training would be after they had been in the Unit for between four and six months. As Officer 17 put it, by then she would have some experience of investigations and "be better able to make some input into the training, and get more out of it."

Different types of courses and programmes exist for specialist officers. These can be categorised according to their content, focus and participants. They are:
- courses covering serious sexual offences, attended by police only;
- courses covering serious sexual offences and child abuse, attended by police only;
- joint training courses on the investigation of child abuse, attended by police and social workers;
- multi-disciplinary training sessions on child abuse, attended by professionals from a range of agencies concerned with child protection.

Table 7.1 shows that in all Forces more than one type of formal training is in operation. Each type of training is outlined below.

7.3.1 Structure and content of police-only courses

Several Forces conduct police-only training courses for serious sexual offences and/or child abuse. In Lothian and Borders, Strathclyde, and Northern it is mandatory for all WPCs to attend such courses after their probation. Apart from Lothian and Borders, where courses are open to both sexes, no male officers attend. The courses are held annually and the aim is to build up a pool of trained officers to be used as specialist officers. The point at which women officers attend a course varies between and within Forces. Some officers attend almost immediately after completing their probationary period whilst others do not attend until after they have been seconded to a Unit. Refresher courses are run in Northern for women officers who have five to seven years service.

The number of officers attending each course also varies. In Strathclyde for example, fifteen WPCs, representing each Division attend; in Northern ten WPCs attend each course. In Grampian, where there are plans to conduct these courses more than once a year, courses are attended by ten officers of both sexes from different branches of the police. Tayside operates a series of one-off training days each year attended, in addition to CAFSES officers, by male and female officers from the uniformed branch and the CID.

Courses are held in-house at Force training schools, and the training is conducted by police training officers, senior and/or experienced Unit officers and other professionals, such as Procurators Fiscal, police surgeons, paediatricians, forensic scientists, Reporters, social workers and, occasionally, psychologists or psychiatrists. In two Forces, there is training input by Rape Crisis Centres and in Strathclyde only, there is input by representatives from Victim Support Schemes.

In Forces with dedicated facilities for the interviewing of victims, training incorporates visits to these premises and practical instruction on use of the Rape Kits.

Courses vary in duration: for example they last for seven days in Strathclyde, five days in Northern, three days in Lothian and Borders and two days in Grampian.

All courses incorporate common core components although individual course content varies considerably. The main components are:
- the law relating to sexual offences and/or child abuse;
- medical and forensic matters relating to sexual offences and/or child abuse;
- legal-evidential requirements;
- relevant Force or Standing Orders;
- the role of the specialist officer;
- the initial reporting stage;
- the obtaining of statements;
- the medical examination;
- obtaining and care of productions;
- interviewing techniques;
- arrangements with social workers regarding child abuse investigations.

The amount of time and emphasis on each core component varies quite considerably between Forces. For example, in one Force a one-hour session on the physical abuse of children is given by a hospital doctor. In another, the same topic includes sessions by odontologists regarding bite marks, input by a casualty surgeon on burn marks and by a paediatrician on general childhood injuries.

The amount of time allocated to interviewing techniques also varies. One Force devotes two full days to the interviewing of children who may have experienced sexual abuse. Another Force devotes two half-day sessions to interviewing children regarding physical and sexual abuse. One and a half days are allocated to the interviewing of women reporting sexual assault in one course. In another this subject is covered in three hours.

The inclusion of additional training material is discretionary, and again varies from Force to Force. For example, Strathclyde includes information on Rape Trauma Syndrome, the care and welfare of victims and the impact of

TABLE 7.1 Training provision for specialist officers

Force	Joint training for child abuse investigations (police & social workers)	Multi-disciplinary training sessions on child abuse (child protection agencies) 1	Serious sexual offence and child abuse training course (police only)	Serious sexual offence training course (police only)
Central Police Child Protection Unit	5 day course (incl 3 days residential)	All Divisions	-	-
Fife Constabulary Child Protection Unit	5 day course (incl 3 days residential)	All Divisions	-	-
Dumfries and Galloway Police Female and Child Unit	3 day course	All Divisions	-	-
Grampian Police Female and Child Enquiry Section	5 day course	All Divisions	-	2 day course
Lothian & Borders Police Woman and Child Unit	3 day course	some Divisions	3 day course	-
Strathclyde Police Female and Child Unit	2 day course some Divisions	some Divisions	7 day course	-
Tayside Police Child and Female Specialist Enquiry Section	under review		ad hoc 1 day sessions on different topics	-
Northern Constabulary Child Abuse Co-ordinator and Specialist Officers	under review	All Divisions	5 day course (for post probation officers) 5 day refresher course (for officers with 2 - 5 yrs service)	-

1 These may include police, social workers, nurses, health visitors, RSSPCC, GPs, nursery nurses, teachers, representatives from the Procurator Fiscal and Reporter's office.

Source: Force training documents and interviews with officers

violence on women and children. The course in Northern also covers issues relating to the welfare and the well-being of the complainer. In three Forces some information is provided on the long-term effects of child sexual abuse. Some courses also include sessions on ethnic awareness.

Additional training material also reflects the specific remit of each Unit. In Strathclyde for example, the remit of the Female and Child Units extends to cot deaths and training includes information on Sudden Infant Death Syndrome. Apart from Strathclyde, which includes some information on the legislation contained in the Matrimonial Homes (Family Protection) (Scotland) Act 1980, no Force offers any training relating to domestic violence.

Training methods on these courses include formal lectures, informal discussion periods, role-plays of interviews, report writing and, in some cases, video presentation. In Strathclyde, officers are given a comprehensive training manual to take away with them as the end of the course. This manual contains information on a range of issues including police procedure, the role of the Unit, the medical examination, Rape Trauma Syndrome, guidance on statement-taking and case conferences. It also includes specimen statements and extracts from relevant legislation.

Few courses provide officers with lists of agencies offering information, advice or support to victims. Where there is training input by these agencies, written information packs from them are usually provided.

7.3.2 Officers' views of police-only training

Of the fourteen officers interviewed who had experienced police-only courses, approximately half found them helpful and beneficial, and half found the content to be of limited practical use. Those who held the latter view attributed this to the time lapse between undergoing training and doing the work being too great. They had little opportunity to put into practice what they had learnt on the course. Secondly, officers felt that there was an over-emphasis on what they termed "trivial" concerns, such as the use of anatomically correct dolls for disclosure work or "technical" matters, such as the use of small cameras to photograph injuries. They felt that they would never use either of these items. They suggested that courses did not include enough practical information on how to undertake joint investigations, interviewing techniques, especially in relation to children and the writing of reports. Thirdly, they felt that there was an imbalance in the input on the courses, with an emphasis on information relating to adult sexual assault, whilst their work in the Units was largely concerned with child abuse investigations.

7.3.3 Structure and content of joint police/social work training

Joint police/social work training is a relatively recent innovation in Scotland. Central Police and Central Region SWD conducted the first joint course in 1988 and, with slight modifications, they have run an annual course since then with the aim of building up a 'pool' of officers and social workers for the Central CPU. In 1990, officers and social workers from the CPU in Fife attended the second training course run in Central. Grampian and Dumfries and Galloway held joint police/social work courses for the first time in November 1991 and May 1992 respectively, with the intention of repeating them on a regular basis. Lothian and Borders and Strathclyde have also introduced a joint training course. Northern plans to follow suit in the near future.

Joint training courses are organised and run in conjunction with SWDs. They are usually attended by equal numbers of police and social workers. In most courses there is a gender mix from police and social workers. The courses are sometimes attended by members of the social work Emergency Duty Team. Joint courses vary in structure and content, although they share the following common objectives:
- to integrate police and social workers;
- to generate mutual trust and confidence;
- to promote an exchange of information between the two agencies relative to their roles and responsibilities in the investigation of child abuse;
- to educate police and social workers in methods of conducting child protection and child abuse investigations, especially in interviewing techniques.

Focusing on joint arrangements for the investigation of child abuse, the courses emphasise the need for a smoother, swifter and more collaborative response. They have a strong focus on the referral and investigative process and on techniques for interviewing children.

The main organisational goals of the courses are:
- to improve professional relationships between individual police officers and social workers;
- to facilitate professional collaboration and communication;
- to improve decision-making and case management in child abuse investigations.

In all joint courses, instruction is given on law and legal requirements in child abuse investigations and related medical and forensic issues. The emphasis, however, is on the respective statutory roles and complementary responsibilities of both agencies. Input on procedural guidelines, legislation and professional roles and responsibilities is given by police and SWD training officers, senior officers and social work managers and outside speakers, including Procurators Fiscal, Reporters, paediatricians, RSSPCC and police surgeons.

Interviewing skills comprise a large part of each course; training on techniques for interviewing children is given on all courses by outside experts brought in specifically for that purpose. Some courses also include sessions on the experience of abuse from the child's perspective, stages of child development, techniques for communicating with children of different ages and the long-term effects of child abuse.

An important aim of these courses is the generation of respect and trust between agencies. Training therefore includes skill-sharing opportunities, where individuals are encouraged to share information based on their occupational and professional experience and expertise. The training also aims to break down barriers between police and social workers and to dispel the misconceptions and apprehensions which one group has of the other.

All courses include communication exercises which aim to challenge professional stereotypes. To this end, for example, the course in Central includes a three day residential component where officers and social workers are encouraged to socialise after the formal training periods.

Training methods include exercises where social workers and police officers are paired, role-plays of interviews, video presentations and group discussions. In Dumfries and Galloway an innovative part of the training programme is the interviewing of a group of school children on particular events which took place in school the previous day. This exercise is used to give officers the opportunity to talk to children and to gain first-hand experience of how children recall and describe events.

7.3.4 Officers' views of joint police/social work training

There was a range of views from officers regarding these courses. Some gave them fulsome praise, finding the courses "stimulating", "highly informative", "comprehensive" and valuable in terms of meeting and sharing information. They also welcomed the opportunity for developing practice skills.

Other officers found the courses a "mishmash", "just a joke", "too technical" and thought they were "artificial in trying to get us to get along with social workers".

On the whole, however, officers enjoyed learning about the work of social workers, something that most of them admitted they knew little or nothing about prior to the course. They also felt that it was valuable and worthwhile for police and social workers to learn about each others' roles and responsibilities; the training course provided an opportunity to do this.

The main advantage of joint training was felt to be the learning of new skills for interviewing children. The imparting of these skills was aided by practical exercises with social workers who, according to all officers, were better versed in communicating with children than they were. The courses were also felt to be successful in achieving their aim of acquainting police with the roles and responsibilities of social workers. As Officer 14 said,

> "We police tend to have a wee bit blinkered view. I saw the problems from the social worker's side and I realised what has been going wrong between us .... It made me as a police officer take a step back and think about the situation in a broader way".

Another advantage to this type of course was being able to "put a face to a name". All officers maintained they were more confident and at ease about future joint working with social workers they had met on the course. One officer summed it up thus "It has sown the seeds of future trust and respect." He felt that this would go some way to circumventing future problems in joint working.

7.3.5 Multi-disciplinary training sessions

These training sessions are a response to the recommendations made in *Effective Intervention* for closer working relationships between all agencies involved in child protection. They are organised by Area Review/Child Protection Committees in each local authority region and they provide a forum for workers from a variety of professions to come together. Police, social workers, RSSPCC, doctors, health visitors, paediatricians and casualty surgeons, teachers, Procurators Fiscal and staff from the Reporter's office are invited to attend. Sessions of a half or full day's duration are held on particular topics including agency responsibilities, emergency procedures, case conferences and the child protection register. The frequency of the training and the range of topics covered varies between regions. All Forces participate in these training sessions.

7.3.6 Officers' views of multi-disciplinary training sessions

Most officers found these training sessions helpful, especially when they were attended by other professionals working in the same geographical area. They were less helpful when they were attended by workers from different locations. As Officer 8 noted,

> "What is the point of meeting these people and trying to build up relationships if you are not even going to be working with them?"

An additional issue relates to attendance at multi-disciplinary training. Many officers said that although they had been scheduled to attend, they were often unable to do so on the day because of pressures of work or urgent police business. This defeated the main purpose of such training: not only were officers missing out on valuable training opportunities, but it was often too late for another officer to take their place, resulting in no police attendance at the session.

7.3.7 The aide system

Lothian and Borders and some Divisions of Strathclyde operate an 'aide' system for Female and Child Unit officers. This is a system of attachment whereby female uniformed officers spend a period of time working in a Unit, gaining practical experience in undertaking enquiries and investigations. In Lothian and Borders, attachment to the Unit as an aide is open to all officers, who must apply for a three month period. Applicants are assessed by their Divisional officer and they undergo an interview. There is a recognised need to ensure that officers selected for the attachment have an interest in the work and that they are not selected on the basis of availability. The aim here is to "build up a pool of suitably experienced officers."[4] In Strathclyde, women uniformed officers from some Divisions are attached for a six-month period to the Divisional Female and Child Unit for the same purpose.

The aide system functions as a learning experience for potential Unit officers, giving them the opportunity to experience the work of a Unit first hand. It is also used as a means for line managers to assess the potential of officers for secondment to a Unit. Officers themselves commented very favourably on the aide system, seeing it as an excellent means of learning about the work of the Units prior to secondment.

7.3.8 The exchange system

A recent development in two Forces (Strathclyde and Dumfries and Galloway) has been the setting up of an 'exchange system' whereby Unit officers and social workers swap workplaces for a period ranging from a day to a week. The aim of this system is to enhance mutual understanding of roles and responsibilities in the investigation of child abuse and to provide practical experience of the extent and limitations of these professional roles. There are no plans to develop the exchange system in other Forces.

7.4   CONCLUSION

There is now a recognition by the police of the importance of training in relation to the investigation of sexual assault and child abuse. Although there is still a strong emphasis on gaining practical experience, formal training now occupies a position of central importance in officers' preparation for working in the Units. All Forces have specific training strategies for specialist officers and in some Forces these training courses are also attended by CID officers. New courses are being introduced and existing courses are continually restructured and expanded to reflect current thinking and incorporate new developments - particularly in the area of child abuse.

Training courses on serious sexual assault now go considerably beyond the relevant legislation and related medical and forensic matters. A major development has been an emphasis on the development of skills for the interviewing of women reporting sexual assault. Several Forces include material about the impact of violence against women, information on Rape Trauma Syndrome and the long-term effects of sexual assault. Training is designed to counteract stereotypical images of women who report rape and to challenge myths about rape. Officers are encouraged to listen to women and not to make assumptions on the basis of her demeanour, dress or circumstances of the assault. Several courses draw attention to the irrelevance of a woman's sexual history, noting that legislation has been passed to limit the admissibility of such evidence in court.[5]

There have also been significant changes in the methods used on training courses. Training is now rarely conducted by means of lectures with little opportunity for question or discussion. There is a greater willingness by some Forces to include outside speakers from voluntary agencies which provide support to those who have experienced sexual assault. Although only one Force (Strathclyde) has developed a comprehensive training manual for officers to take away, this practice could be extended. Manuals can provide useful information on legislation and procedures and can act as effective aide-memoires.

Advances have also been made in the area of child abuse training. In the last four years there has been a major shift in emphasis. Since the first joint training course held in Central in 1988, five other Forces have initiated joint training with social workers. In the remaining Forces, Tayside and Northern, such training is under review. Training is no longer restricted to aspects of policy, investigative procedure and legal-evidential requirements in the gathering of evidence for prosecution. The idea of the police as agents of child protection has gained credence and this is reflected in training which is focused on the welfare of the child.

The inclusion of social workers in the training has led to the adoption of new training methods. They are more participative and include role-playing, simulated interviews and work on hypothetical case studies. Courses are designed to be more reflective, with opportunity for active participation and discussion. Training is also increasingly skills-based, with an emphasis on developing practice skills in the interviewing of children. Scottish

Forces, like their English counterparts, now include input from experts on child sexual abuse from other agencies. The development of multi-agency training sessions has also widened the parameters of police training in the area of child abuse. These sessions provide opportunities for informal discussion and a broadening of perspective for police. They also provide a forum for participants to get to know each other on a more informal basis.

Since the Units were established, there has been less opportunity for uniformed officers to gain general experience of sexual assault and child abuse enquiries. Although it is now recognised that formal training is important and necessary, the long-held belief that "there is no substitute for experience" still dominates police occupational culture. The 'aide system' was developed to enable women officers to gain practical experience of the Units prior to a period of secondment. This system gives officers the opportunity to gain experience and skills in enquiries and also provides them with a better understanding of the nature of work undertaken in the Units. It also equips them with some practical knowledge prior to attending formal training courses. The 'exchange' system also provides the opportunity to gain practical experience. As Waterhouse and Carnie (1990) noted, these exchanges also prepare officers for contributing to in-service training and enable them to advise colleagues on how to liaise with other agencies.[6]

Some formal training courses are routinely attended by CID and uniformed officers but this is not standard practice in all Forces. Even where a Unit exists, it is likely that a women who reports a sexual assault will make initial contact with a uniformed officer who is not based in a specialist Unit. This also applies to CID officers who may be the investigating officers in sexual assault cases. Including CID and uniformed officers on training courses could ensure that these officers would be better equipped to investigate such cases. It would also encourage a better understanding between CID, uniformed officers and specialist officers.

The majority of officers themselves would welcome more training in specific areas including video interviewing, how to avoid asking leading questions and dealing with disturbed children and children with disabilities.

A further point relates to the planning and organisation of police-only and joint training courses. Police training sections, SWDs and working groups with representatives from a range of agencies have all played a part in extending and improving training for investigating crimes of violence against women and children.

Two themes merit consideration in relation to the organisation of training. Firstly, there is evidence that participants for some courses are selected on the basis of their availability for training rather than on the likelihood of working on joint investigations with their police/social work counterpart. This clearly limits the effectiveness of the training. Secondly, there may be a case for appointing inter-agency training staff to co-ordinate and plan the training in a systematic way. Such an appointment has already been made in Central and there are proposals for a similar appointment in Grampian.

Finally, it should be noted that, apart from the legislative information given on Strathclyde training courses, there is no specialist training on domestic violence. Most Forces are currently reviewing their policies on the police response to domestic violence. It is important for officers to receive training which sensitises them to the needs of women who are victims of such violence before the implementation of new policing strategies in this area.

Footnotes

---

1   Chambers, G and Millar, A. (1983).
2   CC Circular 7/1985.
3   Home Office Circular 52/1985; DDHSS (1988) Working Together; SWSG (1989) Effective Intervention;
4   Lothian and Borders Standing Order 21/88.
5   ss141a/141b & ss346A/346B Criminal Procedure (Scotland)Act 1975 as inserted by s36 Law Reform (Miscellaneous Provisions) (Scotland) Act 1985.
6   Waterhouse, 1. and Carnie, J. (1990).

CHAPTER 8

THE ROLE AND FUNCTION OF SPECIALIST UNITS

This Chapter identifies the original aims and objectives of the Units as a starting point for examining the way in which they currently operate. Starting with a brief description of the Units as conceived by policy-makers, the Chapter then outlines the main organisational goals envisaged for them. It also outlines the role and function of the Units in terms of the crimes and offences they deal with and the degree of involvement that specialist officers have in investigations.

8.1 <u>AIMS AND OBJECTIVES OF THE UNITS</u>

The main aim of policy-makers in setting up specialist Units was to improve the police response to victims of sexual assault and child abuse. Units which deal with both sexual assault and child abuse were intended to offer help, advice and support to victims and to undertake certain aspects of the investigative process. A second major objective was to improve working relations and maintain a close liaison with other agencies. CPUs were formed with a different framework. They were to give help and support to victims of child abuse, have policies for joint working with social workers and aimed to provide a co-ordinated approach to child protection. Their objective was to reduce the trauma of the investigation for the victim by developing a more child-centred approach. Liaison with all other agencies concerned with child protection was also to be developed and maintained.

8.2 <u>ORGANISATIONAL GOALS</u>

There were common organisational goals for Units with a dual responsibility for adult sexual assault and child abuse. These were:

- to encourage more women to report crimes of sexual violence by providing a more sympathetic approach to victims;
- to obtain more comprehensive statements from women and children through a more specialist approach;
- to improve the quality of evidence for securing a conviction;
- to provide assistance to the CID.

The CPUs also had specific organisational goals. These were:

- to encourage an inter-agency approach to child protection, so that police were informed about suspected cases at an early stage;
- to reduce the number of unnecessary interviews and medical examinations of a child;
- to improve the quality of evidence to secure a conviction;
- to encourage uniformed officers to report cases of suspected child abuse;
- to devise more accurate methods for recording information on allegations of child abuse.

Table 8.1 Types of crimes and offences dealt with by specialist officers

Force	Rape and attempted Rape	Assault with intent to Rape	Indecent Assault	Indecent Exposure	Lewd & Lib Practices	Sexual Offences (S) Act s3 [1]	Sexual Offences (S) Act s4 [2]	Sexual Offences (S) Act s5 [3]	Incest	Physical Abuse	Sexual Abuse	Neglect	Cot Death	Domestic Violence	Concealment of Pregnancy
Central CP Unit					*	*	*	*	*	*	*		*		
Fife CP Unit					*				*	*	*				
Dumfries and Galloway F&C Unit	*	*	*	*	*	*	*	*	*	*	*				*
Grampian F&C Enquiry Section	* Discretionary	* Discretionary			*				*	*	*				
Lothian & Borders W&C Unit	*	*	* if serious		* if serious				*	* if serious	*			under consideration	
Strathclyde [4] F&C Unit	*	*	*	*	*	*	*	*	*	*	*		*	* one div only	
Tayside CAFSES	*	*	* if serious	* if serious	* if serious	*	*	*	*	*	*			under consideration	
Northern Specialist Officers	*	*	*	*	*	*	*	*	*	*	*	*			

1 Unlawful sexual intercourse with a girl under 13 years.
2 Unlawful sexual intercourse with a girl under 16 years.
3 Indecent behaviour towards a girl between 12 and 16 years.
4 Strathclyde units have an additional remit to deal with all crimes involving female members of an ethnic minority.

Source: Force documents, Force Orders and interviews with officers.

Table 8.2   Stated role and function of Units

Force	Role and Function of Units in investigations
Central Child Protection Unit	Officers from the CPU and social workers from Social Work Area Offices jointly investigate all cases of child abuse from beginning to end. They arrange and attend medical exams and interview all witnesses and offer help and support for victims and their families and attend case conferences. They also deal with cot deaths. Suspect interviews undertaken by police only.
Fife Child Protection Unit	Officers and social workers work from the same location. They offer help and support for victims and their families and attend case conferences. They make enquiries and jointly investigate from beginning to end all cases of child physical and sexual abuse, with the exception of cases of neglect, abandonment, and under-age sex. Suspect interviews undertaken by police only.
Dumfries and Galloway Female and Child Unit	Officers undertake enquiries and investigate fully all cases of child abuse and sexual assault. They give help, advice and support to all victims of sexual assault and child abuse,obtain statements, arrange and attend medical examinations, obtain productions/samples, take necessary photographs, liaise with other agencies and, in the case of children, attend case conferences.
Grampian Police Female and Child Enquiry Section	Officers are responsible for the investigation of child abuse from initial stage to end stage. They undertake interviews, arrange medical examinations, liaise with other agencies and attend case conferences. At the discretion of the DCI officers may also assist CID in cases of rape and serious sexual assault by obtaining statements and arranging medical examinations. Officers may also, depending on the nature of the case and at the discretion of the DCI undertake investigations of other less serious sexual offences eg. some indecent assaults, indecent behaviour.
Lothian and Borders Woman and Child Unit	Officers assist CID by giving help, advice and support to victims of rape, assault with intent to ravish, incest and serious sexual offences. They obtain victim statements, arrange and attend at the medical examination to obtain productions/samples and take photographs if necessary. Officers fully investigate and report cases of child abuse, they offer help and support, arrange and attend medical examinations, liaise with other agencies and attend case conferences. They may also deal with 'vulnerable' witnesses in other crimes.
Strathclyde Female and Child Units	Officers give help and support to victims of sexual assault. In serious cases they assist CID, by obtaining statements and arranging and attending medical examinations and obtaining productions. In less serious offences eg. indecent exposure and some cases of indecent assault, they undertake the entire investigation. Officers also assist CID in cases of child sexual abuse and serious cases of child physical abuse, obtaining statements, and organising medical examinations. They undertake investigations in less serious cases of child abuse. They also deal with cot deaths.
Tayside Child and Female Specialist Enquiry Section (CAFSES)	Officers have a responsibility for the care of female victims of rape and sexual assault and provide assistance to the CID by obtaining statements, arranging and attending at medical examinations and obtaining productions. Officers have an investigative and support role in child abuse investigations. They undertake all investigations from beginning to end, offer support and advice to the child and the child's family, liaise with other child protection agencies and attend case conferences.
Northern Child Abuse Co-ordinator and Specialist Officers	Child Abuse Coordinator is responsible for overseeing all child abuse cases, attending case conferences, liasing with other agencies, and maintaining the 'at risk register'. Specialist officers across Force area undertake investigations of child abuse and sexual assault. In serious cases, this will be in a support capacity to CID, obtaining statements and arranging and attending medical examinations. In less serious cases, eg. minor indecencies and assaults, they undertake the entire investigation.

Source:Force Orders and interviews with policy-makers and Unit officers

8.3   CRIMES AND OFFENCES DEALT WITH BY SPECIALIST OFFICERS

Table 8.1 shows the range of crimes and offences dealt with in each Unit. Some Units investigate the full range of sexual crimes and child abuse. Others deal with a more restricted range of crimes and offences. In these Forces, the 'less serious' offences such as indecent exposure and lesser forms of non-accidental injury to children are dealt with by uniformed officers. The possibility of specialist officers dealing with such cases, however, is not totally excluded. It is dependent, for example, on the workload of the Units and the discretion of senior officers. The CPUs represent a high level of specialisation, concentrating exclusively on child abuse. In Forces where they have been established, the investigation of serious adult sexual crime continues to be undertaken by the CID, assisted by WPCs. Less serious sexual assault is dealt with by uniformed officers.

8.4   DEGREE OF INVOLVEMENT IN INVESTIGATIONS

Table 8.2 shows the stated functions of each Unit, the role played by specialist officers in their work and aspects of the investigation in which these officers are involved.

The working relationship between the specialist officers and the CID differs from Force to Force. In some Forces specialist officers undertake the entire investigation, including the apprehension of the suspect; in others they play a more peripheral role, dealing with the victim only and assisting the CID. The degree of involvement of specialist officers in investigations depends on two factors:

-    the type of crime or offence that is reported;

-    the degree of seriousness of that crime or offence.

These factors are discussed below in relation to the investigation of sexual assault and child abuse.

8.4.1   Role and function in relation to sexual assault

All specialist officers offer advice and support to victims of sexual assault, although the extent of their involvement in investigations varies. With the exception of Dumfries and Galloway, where officers undertake the entire investigation, specialist officers play a supporting role to Divisional CID investigating officers in cases of rape, attempted rape, assault with intent to rape and other serious sexual assaults. The CID investigating officer is in charge of the investigation in terms of the detection of the offender and the reporting of the case to the Procurator Fiscal.

The role of the specialist officer is to gather evidence from and care for the victim. They obtain initial statements from victims, undertake follow-up interviews, arrange and attend medical examinations and other police procedures such as identification parades. They liaise with CID investigating officers and provide a link between the victim and that officer. In the case of less serious sexual offences such as indecent behaviour and minor indecent assaults, Unit officers have a larger role, which may include the apprehension and cautioning of a suspect.

8.4.2   Role and function in relation to child abuse

All Units have a remit for the investigation of child abuse. In most Forces, the development and maintenance of a co-ordinated approach to child abuse was stated as part of the general function of the Units. A formally stated policy of joint working operates in the CPUs. Inter-agency arrangements regarding joint arrangements between Unit officers and social workers differ significantly between and within Forces and this is discussed in Chapter 11.

In most Forces, specialist officers undertake child abuse investigations from the point of initial referral to the eventual outcome of the case. They make enquiries and undertake all aspects of investigations, including the reporting of the case to the relevant authorities such as the Procurator Fiscal and the Reporter to the Children's Panel. In the majority of cases, investigations are undertaken by specialist officers without the involvement of Divisional CID. Consequently, Units have a relatively higher level of autonomy in relation to the CID in child abuse cases than they do in the investigation of sexual assault.

In certain circumstances, however, specialist officers may work alongside Divisional CID officers. This happens where the investigation is particularly complex or serious, perhaps involving a group of perpetrators or a serial child abuser. In such cases the detection, apprehension and interviewing of the suspect is usually carried out by CID officers who are also responsible for reporting the case. The specialist officer works under the direction of the CID officer and is responsible for interviewing the child and other witnesses, arranging and attending case conferences, maintaining contact with other agencies and providing support to the child and the child's family throughout the investigation.

8.4.3 Role and function in relation to domestic violence

During the period of the research, domestic violence was not part of the remit of the specialist Units. These investigations were routinely handled in each Force by uniformed officers. In mid-1991, however, a 'domestic violence initiative' was undertaken by one Unit in Strathclyde. This was originally intended as a six month pilot study to record the incidence of 'domestic call-outs', and to assess the feasibility of all Units in the Force responding to domestic violence. At the end of the pilot period the initiative was extended indefinitely in this one Unit only.

The initiative operates in the following way: uniformed officers (predominantly male), routinely attend incidents of domestic violence. Whilst in the home, officers inform the woman that members of the Female and Child Unit will call on her within a week. They give her a card with details about the local Victim Support Scheme. Thereafter, two Unit officers, or a Unit officer and a uniformed female officer, call at the woman's home and give her an information card with the telephone numbers of the SWD, the Housing Department, the Unit and the local Women's Aid group. Verbal information about Court Orders and Interim Interdicts is also given to the woman. On their own initiative, Unit officers also give information and the contact number of a local women's counselling and resource centre and an Asian women's support group. If the woman is not at home, the Unit officers leave a calling card. If she does not call the Unit there is no further follow-up. If she has already reported an incident of domestic violence, however, officers will usually make every effort to see her. Unit officers fill in a form for every visit they make and this is sent to the Divisional administration office for collation.

8.4.4 Other duties

Specialist officers are frequently called upon to undertake other duties. This is particularly the case in 'satellite' Units, Units without a promoted officer, or Units under the direct command of a Divisional CID officer as in Strathclyde. These other duties may include the investigation of cot deaths, accompanying a female suspect to the scene of crime, dealing with missing persons, interviewing abscondees from children's homes and putting data on to the police computer system. Whilst this may be acceptable when officers are not busy, it also means that they are not always available when a call for their specialist services comes in.

8.5   CONCLUSION

The wide variety in remit of the Units, together with their range of investigative functions is evident. Some of the variety is a product of historical factors; in other cases it is due to the degree of specialisation implemented by individual Forces.

CHAPTER 9

THE INVESTIGATION OF SEXUAL ASSAULT

This Chapter describes current police practice following a report of a sexual assault such as rape, attempted rape or indecent assault. It focuses on the role played by specialist officers from the time of initial contact with a woman reporting an assault, throughout any subsequent enquiries and investigation. Particular attention is paid to the interviewing of the complainer. The Chapter draws on material from the data collection exercise (SPU/1 forms) and police interviews. Comparison is made with the findings of Chambers and Millar (1983) regarding aspects of the investigation which were found to be particularly distressing for the complainer. The procedures described here refer to the practice of specialist officers in Northern Constabulary and the five Forces that have dual-responsibility Units.[1] They do not refer to practice in Central Police and Fife Constabulary.

9.1 REPORTS OF SEXUAL ASSAULT : THE DATA

During the-four month data collection period, specialist officers were asked to record details of all reports and requests for police assistance in which they were involved, whether or not a criminal investigation ensued. They recorded their involvement in a total of 898 enquiries, 136 (15%) of which were reports of sexual assault. Table 9.1 shows the numbers and types of all enquiries in which specialist officers were involved.

Table 9.1 Cases in which specialist officers were involved

Force	Total cases	Child abuse	Adult sexual assault	Domestic violence	Other *
Central CPU	122	122 (100)	- (-)	- (-)	- (-)
Fife CPU[1]	58	54 (93)	- (-)	- (-)	4 (7)
Dumfries & Galloway[2]	27	22 (82)	5 (19)	- (-)	- (-)
Grampian	57	46 (81)	11 (19)	- (-)	- (-)
Lothian & Borders	191	155 (81)	34 (18)	2 (1)	- (-)
Northern[3]	33	30 (91)	1 (3)	- (-)	2 (6)
Strathclyde	387	279 (72)	65 (17)	** (**)	43(11)
Tayside[4]	23	2 (9)	20 (87)	1 (4)	- (-)
Total	898	710 (79)	136 (15)	3 (1)	49 (5)

Numbers in brackets represent percentages in each Force.

* The 'other category' includes enquiries that were not strictly classifiable under the other listed categories and include reports of indecent exposure, 'flashing', receiving indecent mail and telephone calls, dealing with missing person enquiries, dealing with cases of under-age pregnancies, cot-death enquiries and interviewing abscondees from childrens' homes.

** Not included here are those cases dealt with under the 'domestic violence initiative' in one Unit in Strathclyde, total number of which was 99.

1   At the time of this exercise only one CPU was in operation in Fife, covering one police Division.
2   Unit in Dumfries & Galloway was very newly incepted, with only one specialist officer in post at this time.
3   Forms filled in by specialist officers in selected areas only, ie Inverness, Dingwall, Tain, Aviemore, Nairn and Benbecula.
4   In Tayside, it was only possible to use the data collection form to record cases of adult sexual assault. The two cases here refer to reports by adults of past abuse during chilhood.

Table 9.2 provides a breakdown of allegations in the 136 reports of sexual assault dealt with by specialist officers during the data collection period. It is not possible to say whether this figure represents all reports made to the police during this period.[2] Neither can it be certain that all enquiries dealt with by specialist officers during the period were recorded for the research.[3]

Table 9.2   Type of allegation dealt with by specialist officers

Force	Rape	Attempted rape	Assault with intent to rape	Indecent assault	Total
Grampian	6	2	-	3	11
Northern	-	-	-	1	1
Dumfries & Galloway	4	-	-	1	5
Lothian & Borders	23	5	1	5	34
Tayside	6	4	3	7	20
Strathclyde	29	9	8	19	65
Total	68	20	12	36	136

Allegations of rape accounted for exactly half of all reports of sexual assault dealt with by specialist officers. Indecent assaults accounted for a quarter (26%) of reports, attempted rape accounted for 15% and assault with intent to ravish accounted for 9%. Specialist officers usually classified the incident using the complainer's own definition of what happened, although interviews revealed that at least some incidents were re-defined by officers into a different crime category, particularly those classified as attempted rape and or assault with attempt to ravish.[4]

9.2   REPORTING A SEXUAL ASSAULT

9.2.1   Notifying specialist officers

All Forces have specific procedures for notifying Units when a report of sexual assault is made to the police. These are outlined in Force instructions. Taking account of distance and geographical factors, the notification procedures are similar in each Force. As soon as a report of a serious sexual assault is received, the CID are immediately informed and they alert the Unit. In some Forces the Unit is located close to the CID office. In others, however, the Divisional DCI will contact the Unit or, in the case of Northern, the specialist officer stationed at the nearest police station. Most Force instructions emphasise the requirement that Units are notified of serious sexual assaults as soon as possible to ensure that specialist officers reach the complainer at an early stage. As in all other areas of police work, investigations are overseen by a senior officer who makes the final decision on whether to refer a case to the Procurator Fiscal.

9.2.2   The allocation of cases

The allocation of cases to specialist officers is done on the basis of existing caseload or on a rota system. Where there are promoted officers in post in a Unit they are responsible for the internal division of labour. In other Units, allocation of cases is usually done by the DCI on the basis of the availability of specialist officers. Where there is no night-shift cover, officers are called out on a rota system by the duty officer.

Once allocated, the specialist officer remains attached to the case, providing continuity and acting as a link with the complainer throughout the enquiry. They are responsible for providing support to the complainer and assisting the CID until the investigation is complete. At times during the enquiry, the specialist officer may be assisted by other Unit officers.

Chambers and Millar (1983) found that contact with a number of officers to whom she repeated what had happened was distressing for women reporting sexual assault. The allocation of one officer to each case is a means of preventing this distress.

9.2.3 How reports of sexual assault were made

It was found that most reports (59%) were made during the late evening or early hours of the morning. This finding is consistent with previous research.[5] In most cases a specialist officer was called out to give assistance. In 63% of cases, the woman contacted the police directly, either in person or by telephone. Table 9.3 shows the sources of reports of sexual assault.

Table 9.3 Source of reports of sexual assault

Source	%
Complainer	63
Relatives	12
Friends/neighbours	5
Strangers[1]	7
Discovered by local police	3
Medical services[2]	8
Area social workers	2

1 Strangers include passers-by, taxi-drivers, and anonymous callers who contacted the police.
2 Medical services include GPs, hospital casualty surgeons and hospital social workers.

9.2.4 Initial police contact

All specialist officers, except those in Northern Constabulary, are located in Units which are based at Divisional or Sub-Divisional police headquarters. Unless a report of sexual assault is made at one of these locations, it is unlikely that a woman's first contact with the police is with a specialist officer.

When a report of a sexual assault is made at a local police station, or to a beat officer, initial contact is with a uniformed officer. The CID and Unit are notified soon after. Similarly, if a complaint is made by means of an emergency telephone call, it is likely that a local uniformed officer will be dispatched to the woman, whilst a call goes out alerting the CID and the Unit.

SHHD guidelines state that from the stage of first reporting the woman should be treated 'with tact, understanding and full regard to her well-being.'[6]   This is reiterated in most Force Orders, which state that any immediate questioning of the woman by uniformed officers should be with a view to identifying the alleged offender and getting brief details of what happened and where it happened.   They also state that such questioning should be conducted in a private setting.

If the woman requires medical attention for injuries, she will be transported to the nearest hospital casualty department accompanied, if possible, by a woman uniformed officer or the officer who first received the report.   If the woman is not injured, the uniformed officer stays with her or escorts her to the police station to await the arrival of the specialist officer. If there is a Unit in the area, the woman may be taken straight there.

When a call comes in to specialist officers the amount of verbal information they receive about the case can vary a great deal.   It ranges from "female, mid 20's, distraught, dirty, torn clothes, flagged down panda car" to much more detailed information about the woman - her age, address, demeanour and a full description of the alleged assault, where it took place, events that led up to it and the name of the assailant. To receive such full information is relatively rare, however, and officers are usually only given brief details.

9.2.5   Delay in contact with specialist officer

All specialist officers try to make contact with the woman as soon as possible, by going to her or arranging for her to be brought into the Unit or interview suite. When a woman is not brought into a Unit, specialist officers may have to negotiate their own transport arrangements.   As indicated in Chapter 5, this can cause considerable inconvenience.   Geographical factors also affect the time taken by a specialist officer to reach a woman.   Where Units cover a large territorial Division, it may be difficult to reach some areas.   This may increase the delay between the time of reporting an assault and contact with a specialist officer.   One consequence of this delay is that a woman experiences prolonged interaction with uniformed officers.

The perceived seriousness of the incident is also an important factor accounting for the length of time between reporting and making contact with a specialist officer. This is particularly so if the report is made at night. Some reports of indecent assaults may not trigger immediate notification procedures and these incidents may be dealt with by uniformed officers. They take details of the incident and inform the Unit the next day. Any follow-up, including more detailed statement-taking will then be done by a specialist officer. The Unit may also become informed of the incident via the 'incident log' which catalogues all incidents reported in a Division over a 24-hour period. Unit officers check this information every day to ascertain any incidents reported overnight that may require attention or follow-up action the following day.

Another factor which may affect the length of time before a woman comes into contact with a specialist officer concerns the time lapse between the incident and the report. The police response is swifter where reports are made soon after an incident and there is the possibility of corroboration through medical or forensic evidence. Table 9.4 shows the length of time between the report first being made and the time when the specialist officer comes into contact with the woman making the report.

Table 9.4   Time between reporting and contact with specialist officer

Time	Number of cases	%
Within 1 hour	70	52
1 to 2 hours	29	21
2 to 3 hours	11	8
3 to 4 hours	8	6
Next day	18	13

In more than half of the cases, the specialist officer made contact with the woman within one hour of the report coming to the attention of the police. This included 64% of rape reports. In nine of the cases where contact was made the following day the report was classified as an indecent assault by a stranger. Examples include:

Case 7916 : woman alleged taxi driver indecently assaulted her by fondling her breasts and making indecent suggestions.

Case 7817 : woman was out running and man naked from waist down jumped out, grabbed her arms and breasts and tried to pull her into bushes before running off.

Case 7614 : woman in car park when man approaches, drops pants and trousers and pushes erect penis against woman and runs off.

The time lapse between reporting an incident and coming into contact with a specialist officer was also longer where the report was made during the night, particularly in Forces (or Divisions) where there were no specialist officers on night-shift.

9.3   FIRST STAGE OF INVESTIGATION

Chambers and Millar (1983) noted that investigations take place in two stages. If the woman is not in need of immediate medical treatment for injuries, enquiries begin with the arrival of the specialist officer. Fifteen of the eighteen specialist officers interviewed said that the first thing they do on coming into contact with the complainer is to explain who they are and the procedures that the woman will be required to undergo during the subsequent investigation. As Officer 4 explained,

> "I tell her what to expect. It's only fair. They are usually tired and the worse for wear, and I don't want to add to her confusion ... I explain who I am, and who the CID are and what we need from her. I explain briefly about the statement and about the medical exam, and why she can't wash and about the need for evidence and that."

Chambers and Millar (1983) also noted the importance of the first interview for establishing rapport between the woman and the investigating officer.[7] Several officers have constructed a preamble to introduce themselves, explain procedures and the need for the woman to relate exactly what happened in as much detail as possible. An assurance is also given that the officer will not be shocked at what the woman has to say. As Officer 11 pointed out,

> "No matter what she has to tell me, I won't be shocked. I have heard just about everything there is to hear, and I try and assure her of that. It's essential that she gets over her embarrassment enough to be able to tell me what happened in her own words."

At this stage the woman is also given the opportunity to contact a friend or relative. Specialist officers will do this on the woman's behalf.

The exact order of enquiries in an investigation of sexual assault depends on the nature and circumstances of each case. Information from the victim about what has occurred helps to inform the order and direction of enquiries. For this reason specialist officers try to obtain details, however brief, of what occurred, before proceeding with other necessary police procedures or practical tasks involving the complainer. Information regarding the locus of the incident, possible witnesses and the offender is relayed by the specialist officer to the CID investigating officer, who has had minimal contact with the complainer at this stage.

Thereafter, several practical tasks involving the complainer may have to be undertaken. Every attempt is made to keep these to a minimum during the first stage of the investigation, with only the most essential in terms of the gathering of evidence carried out. For example, it may be necessary that the woman returns to the locus of the incident in order to describe what happened. In such cases the woman will be accompanied by the specialist officer. She may have to be finger-printed and if this is the case she is again accompanied by the specialist officer.

9.3.1 Early clear-up of cases

It has been pointed out that not all incidents reported to the police become the subject of a criminal investigation.[8] After initial enquiries some cases may be 'cleared up' although they are overseen by a DS for a final decision on whether to report them to the Procurator Fiscal. There are a number of reasons for this, including insufficient evidence, lack of corroboration, the woman does not want to continue with the complaint or there is suspicion by the police about the veracity of the woman's account. During the study period, 21% of cases dealt with by specialist officers were 'cleared up' in this way. The following extracts from the SPU/1 forms filled in by specialist officers illustrate these cases:

Case 9099 : Victim maintained that she had been raped two weeks prior to report of same, but insisted she wished no police action as she felt this would make matters worse. Appeared only to want to talk to someone about this and had been unable to get hold of Rape Crisis.

Case 8006 : Complainer is an informal patient at .... Hospital since 1986 due to her being para-suicidal. She often makes allegations but never before of a sexual nature. She is on a variety of drugs including valium and anti-depressants, and is a very moody person. Her allegation is not corroborated by any injuries nor the fact that she never informed anybody for several hours. The alleged incident was supposed to have taken place on the driveway within the Hospital, which is well-lit, but the complainer maintains it was dark. Her clothing was supposed to have been pulled at but on examining same it appeared intact with no tears or dirt present. There would appear to be no substance to the allegation."

Case 5221 : Allegation of verbal abuse and rape by estranged husband. Estranged husband currently resides out of country and returns very occasionally. There appears to be a history behind the circumstances, and victim is seeking a divorce. Insufficient evidence for any charges.

9.4 MEDICAL EXAMINATIONS

Forensic and medical evidence is very important at the first stage of the investigation, particularly if sexual intercourse or attempted sexual intercourse has been alleged. The co-operation of the complainer is required for all medical examinations. The SHHD guidelines (1985) recommended that arrangements should be made for the complainer to be medically examined in all cases where rape is alleged, and that in other complaints of sexual assault the case for a medical examination should be carefully weighed. The decision to conduct a medical examination depends very much on the circumstances of the case. Formally, this decision rests with the investigating officer. According to specialist officers, however, the decision is made on the basis of what the woman has told them and they usually advise the investigating officer of the need for a medical. Several officers said that they advise the complainer to undergo a medical examination for all types of sexual assaults.

The majority of officers said that they always explain the need for medical examinations to the complainer. Only two of the officers interviewed said that they would not do so. One officer thought women were "already aware" that a medical would have to take place. A second said,

"most of them [complainers] are so far gone at that stage that they don't care, they just go along with it."

This officer also went on to say that she would not think of asking whether a woman would prefer a female doctor, even though there were female police surgeons available.

9.4.1 Contacting police surgeons

Specialist officers contact police surgeons and make arrangements for the medical examination. Arrangements for medicals differ between and within Forces. Some officers expressed strong dissatisfaction with current arrangements. The length of time they have to wait for a police surgeon, geographical distance from the examination and length of time taken to transport a complainer to the examination were all identified as problematic.

The availability of police surgeons at particular times of the day was also put forward as a reason for the delay in conducting medical examinations. This was particularly the case in some Divisions of Tayside, Grampian and Strathclyde. Officers in Lothian and Borders reported that arrangements with police surgeons had improved due to a well-organised rota system for calling them out.

Another source of dissatisfaction concerns the lack of female police surgeons in some Forces. As a result, officers are still unable to offer the complainer a choice of a male or female police surgeon, as recommended in the SHHD guidelines.

Some officers contact a police surgeon as soon as they are notified of a case. Others prefer to wait until they have met with the woman before contacting the police surgeon. All officers said they like to have some information to convey to the police surgeon in advance of him or her meeting the woman. This is done to save time, to avoid the woman having to repeat her story and to direct the police surgeon to injuries which may corroborate or contradict the complainer's account. As Officer 7 explained,

> "Once I have a basis of what happened, I'll call the doctor and say 'I have a twenty five year old girl, it happened six hours ago, she has been assaulted in .... different areas of her body.' So I can tell him when he comes, he knows exactly where to take his samples. When we go into the medical, I've got to be able to say to the doctor 'she scratched him' so he'll know to take nail clippings and scrapings. Or 'he touched her on her chest area' so he takes a swab from her chest area. So if I can tell him all the different areas that have been in contact with this assailant, he knows where to concentrate his examination."

Most officers try to organise medical examinations at the earliest possible opportunity. This is to preserve evidence and, as one officer put it, to "get it over with as soon as possible so that [the complainer] can wash and get more comfortable." (Officer 3)

9.4.2 Role in medical examinations

Specialist officers are present throughout the medical examination. They accompany and offer support to the complainer and they take care of the material evidence gathered during the examination.[9] All samples, swabs and slides collected by the police surgeon are handed over to the specialist officer who will bag, seal and label the samples and arrange for their delivery to police forensic laboratories for analysis. A 'Rape Kit' is used for this purpose.

At the medical examination the complainer's clothes are removed, handed over to the specialist officer and retained for forensic analysis. After the medical examination the complainer is allowed to wash and, if the medical takes place at an interview suite, the shower facilities are used for this purpose. Officers noted that shower facilities are rarely used, women preferring to bath at home. Interview suites also have terry cloth gowns for the use of complainers whose clothes have been retained. Where medical examinations take place at a hospital or doctor's surgery, there appears to be no provision for re-clothing the complainer.

Medical examinations were conducted in 56 of the 136 cases reported to the police (41%). In three cases (one of rape, two of indecent assault) there had been a medical examination before the police became involved. In five cases, the complainers refused to undergo a medical examination.

Table 9.5   Medical examinations in sexual assault cases

Force	Total reports	Medical examinations		
		Rape	Att rape/ Awir[1]	Indecent Assault
Dumfries and Galloway	5	3	-	1
Grampian	11	2	-	1
Lothian and Borders	34	12	5	-
Northern	1	-	-	-
Strathclyde	65	19	5	3
Tayside	20	1	3	1
Total	136	37	13	6

[1] Awir = Assault with intent to rape

In all cases in the sample, the woman underwent one medical examination, either before or after police involvement in the case.   This contrasts with the findings of Chambers and Millar (1983) who found that almost one third of their sample underwent a second medical examination at a later stage.[10]

9.4.3   Timing of medical examination

In this study 46 of the 56 medical examinations took place during the first stage of the investigation.   The remainder took place the following day. Five of these were cases of indecent assault and five were reports of rape. Table 9.6 notes the length of time between contact with a specialist officer and the time of the medical examination.

Table 9.6   Timing of medical examinations

Timing	Rape	Other sexual assault *
Under 1 hour	2	-
1 - 2 hours	13	4
2 - 3 hours	9	7
3 - 4 hours	4	-
4 - 5 hours	3	-
over 5 hours	2	2
Following day	5	5
Total	38	18

* includes attempted rape, assault with intent to rape and indecent assault.

The majority (70%) of medical examinations took place within four hours of coming into contact with the specialist officer.   This did not, however, take account of the time between reporting an incident to the police and contact with a specialist officer.

9.4.4 Site of medical examinations

SHHD guidelines (1985) recommended that medical examinations should be conducted in a 'proper clinical environment so as to reduce stress and produce an atmosphere of care and concern.'

Table 9.7   Site of medical examinations

Hospital	21
GP surgery	3
Medical room in interview suite	24
Police office medical room	8
Total	56

The majority of examinations in this study (85%) took place in a hospital, a doctor's surgery or the special medical examination room in an 'interview suite' in a Unit. Tayside and Dumfries and Galloway are the only Forces in which medical examinations are conducted in police office medical rooms that are not for the sole use of victims of sexual assault or child abuse. These rooms are in Force or Divisional Headquarters or a local police station.

Chambers and Millar (1983) found that, with very few exceptions, medical examinations took place in local police station or Divisional Headquarters, where facilities were poorly rated by police surgeons and ill-equipped in terms of the necessary medical instruments.

The findings of this study indicate that the majority of examinations are now taking place in well equipped premises which provide a 'proper clinical environment'.

9.5   DURATION OF FIRST STAGE OF INVESTIGATION

The first stage of the investigation involves initial contact with the specialist officer and a statement about what happened. In some cases this stage is very brief, and requires taking a fuller statement at the second stage of the investigation.

Table 9.8   Duration of first stage of investigation

Duration	%
Under half an hour	6
0.5 - 1 hour	28
1 - 2 hours	28
2 - 3 hours	20
3 - 4 hours	9
4 - 5 hours	8
Over 5 hours	1

In some cases, police involvement is completed at this stage. This is because the offender has been detected, the complaint is withdrawn by the complainer, or because the police believe that there is insufficient evidence to proceed with the investigation. The following are examples of cases which were completed after the first stage of investigations.

Case 5220: Offender apprehended in pub and he admitted the assault. Report to Fiscal. No further police action.

Case 4009: Due to victim's medical condition (Huntingdons Chorea) and after consultation with her GP who states she is already slightly demented, it was believed that the [rape] allegation was false.

Case 8007: Complainer alleging she was out for the evening with two friends for a drink. She consumed approx six gins in the evening. Thereafter she left the pub and got a private taxi home alone. She then states that whilst in the taxi, the driver raped her. On further questioning she then stated that the taxi driver tried to kiss her, he then sat astride her and tried to put his hand up her skirt. She pushed him away and he took her home. A medical was carried out which revealed it was her menstrual cycle and there was no evidence of recent injuries or bruises or forcible penetration. It was felt that the complainer was not telling the truth and this was put to her.

Case 9031: Allegation of rape by an acquaintance. Allegation withdrawn by complainer (aged 17) on advice of her parents who thought it would be in her best interests, contrary to police advice.

9.6   THE STATEMENT INTERVIEW

An important aspect of the work of specialist officers is the obtaining of a statement from the complainer. The timing of this depends on the circumstances of the case. Officers said that although they prefer to get a detailed statement from the woman as early as possible, this depends on the condition of the woman. Most officers said they tried to assess how much the woman is able to relate and in what detail, before attempting to obtain a full statement. A number of factors are weighed up. These include the time of day, how long the woman has been waiting for the arrival of the specialist officer, whether the woman has consumed alcohol and how distressed she is. As Officer 6 noted,

> "Initially you've got to tread quite warily with the kind of questions to ask until you get an impression of the person, and how they are reacting to the kinds of questions you are asking. Before I ask any questions at all I introduce myself and explain exactly the procedure we are going through and why we are going through it. I might even take them round and show them the different rooms in the suite so they know why it's happening and then they don't have to ask questions of me once I start asking about some of the more intimate details of what happened. Usually from that point I start to get an idea about whether they are able to speak to me or not and how I think they might get on as we go through the actual statement, as it can be quite a lengthy process."

The statement interview is undertaken by the specialist officer in private with the complainer. It can take place in the interview suite or in the complainer's home and it may be interrupted by the arrival of the police surgeon to undertake the medical examination. If this is the case, the interview may be resumed after the examination or the next day.

Two thirds of specialist officers said they would always ask a complainer if she wished a friend or third party to be present with her during the interview. Some officers said they found the presence of someone else distracting, preferring to interview the complainer alone. Other officers like to have a second specialist officer sitting in on the interview. In some cases, the CID investigating officer may decide to be present for part or all of the interview although, apart from asking some clarifying questions, the interview is generally conducted by the specialist officer.

Several officers said they were 'territorial' about their work with the complainer, particularly for the statement interview. As Officer 6 pointed out,

"We get quite selfish about [the statement interview] in the Unit. Because once we get to that person, no one else is allowed to intrude. And once the person is taken into the suite, then the door is closed. And no one is allowed to get in. And we relate the story to the CID officer who is in charge of the enquiry. They will only speak to that woman about very basic details, and we usually try and work it that they only speak to her through ourselves."

9.6.1 Features of the interview

Chambers and Millar (1983) reported that complainers had negative views of their interactions with CID and uniformed officers in the course of interviewing. Their report described five features of CID interviewing practices which made the interview situation unpleasant for complainers. These were:

- officers' sceptical attitudes;
- a tendency to group incidents into 'good' and 'bad' cases based on the features of the case and the character of the complainer;
- expectations of the complainer's behaviour after the incident;
- requiring higher standards of evidence than required by law;
- interpretations of behaviour seen as constituting consent.

With two exceptions, the officers in this study said that they try to approach each case as objectively as possible, without any presumptions about 'real' rapes or images about 'real' victims. Several officers said that because of these attitudes they had been accused of naivety by non-Unit officers.

Most officers referred to maintaining a balance between their investigative and support role. Officer 1 summed up this view,

"Although sympathetic we have to remain on that middle line. We have to try and evaluate what happened, whilst at the same time trying to give the necessary support."

The main questions which concern specialist officers during the interview are:

- does the woman know her attacker?
- where did the assault happen?
- exactly how did it happen?
- were weapons used?
- are there any possible witnesses who may have seen or heard anything?
- are there any possible witnesses who saw her just before or just after the assault?
- were vehicles involved?

Once a picture of the incident starts to emerge, officers look for corroborating features. In common with the officers interviewed by Chambers and Millar (1983), specialist officers said that any sign of injuries is treated as important corroborating evidence. The state of the woman's clothing is also significant.

Specialist officers did not display such intense preoccupations with the complainer's credibility as the officers interviewed by Chambers and Millar. The consistency of the complainer's account was an important factor to take into consideration, however, in an assessment of the case. As Officer 13 pointed out,

"Obviously you want to make up your mind as soon as you can whether it's a genuine allegation, and that's your own perception of it really. What you are looking for is continuity in the story. We ask her the same sort of questions a few times, just to clear some things."

Officer 1 qualified this by saying that in many cases, inconsistencies in the complainer's story were "usually because she is distressed, and seems to contradict herself." Another officer said that the "ordeal" of the police procedures could contribute to the woman's confusion and bewilderment.

"A lot of woman are absolutely appalled, first of all at what happened to them, then they've got to go to the police and get asked questions, then they are subjected to an internal examination which they have probably never had before, and which I wouldn't fancy myself and ... after this examination they've got to go back and finish their statement. And of course, they are finished, they might be tired, they're upset, they get confused and we are asking them for as many details as we can possibly get. They can get things wrong."

False reporting of sexual assaults was not thought by specialist officers to be common. Nine officers said they had never encountered a false allegation or, as one said "If one was a false complaint, I never realised it, and neither did the Fiscal." Three officers said they had had "suspicions" about "one or two cases" but "generally it's quite rare." These suspicions arose from a belief that what the woman was alleging was not possible given her description of events. Two officers said they had experienced several "spates of false complaints" and referred to some complainers who in their opinion were "mentally disturbed" and who "regularly" made false complaints, "in order to seek attention."

Other officers recalled cases where there were inaccuracies or deliberate omissions in the complainer's account which cast doubt on the allegation, even though they were "sure" it wasn't false. Officer 7 gave the following explanation for this type of occurrence,

"It's unfortunate in that a lot of girls - I'm not saying every girl - but quite a few of them don't perhaps give quite the right story, and it's not that they are telling lies or they are in the wrong. but it's ... I think they feel somehow guilty. Perhaps if they met somebody, if they actually met the assailant that night and went with him, walked home with him or whatever, they maybe feel they shouldn't have done that. Then something has happened, and maybe they feel they don't want to say that they went home with him, and so they don't say it. And I always try to say to them, 'Listen if you had seen this guy, and you quite fancied him, and if you had a wee kiss and a cuddle, tell me about it. Because it won't take any of your credibility away. But if you don't tell me about it and if we find out afterwards or at a later stage, it will take some of your credibility away."

All officers said that the demeanour of the woman when relating what happened is not always an accurate indicator of her distress. All emphasised that women react differently to a sexual assault,

"Some people can suffer the most horrific attacks and are as calm as you like. Some are completely the opposite. But if a woman is claiming she was raped, it gets treated as a rape."
(Officer 4)

"There's no 'normal' reaction as such. Some women are really upset, trembling and distressed, but that's not always the case. They may come in and be very calm about it. And then they might break down at one point, or they may remain dead calm throughout. And then again you may not be able to get anything from her for a couple of days. Or you get a kind of a delayed reaction from her. I am really interested in the story, not really that much in the way it is told." (Officer 16)

73

These views contrast markedly with the views and expectations of CID officers interviewed by Chambers and Millar (1983), who held a more rigid view of how a woman reporting a sexual assault should behave.

9.7   SECOND STAGE OF THE INVESTIGATION

The second stage of the investigation usually begins the following day. If no detailed statement has already been obtained, it is undertaken at this stage. The interview may be undertaken in the complainer's home or the interview suite. This stage of the investigation can extend for several days, with complainers meeting with specialist officers. It may be necessary to photograph injuries or wounds sustained by the complainer and because bruising can take some time to emerge, this is usually done during the second stage of the investigation. Photographs are taken in interview suites by specialist officers using small cameras. In some Forces this is done by police photographers. There were some complaints about the delay in awaiting the arrival of a photographer and it was also noted that, with the exception of Grampian, there are no female photographers who could be used in such cases.

Sometimes complainers are asked to look at books of photographs to see if they recognise their assailant and they may be asked to attend ID parades in order to identify the offender. Most Forces now have improved facilities for the identification of suspects, which involve one-way mirrors. These procedures are arranged by specialist officers, who also accompany the complainer throughout the procedures.

In this study, 47 % of complainers went on to take part in a second stage of investigations. In most cases this stage was confined to taking photographs and clarifying points about the statement. Of these women, 20% had to give a second lengthy and detailed statement to the specialist officer. Five women had a third detailed interview. Three of these women were in Strathclyde and two were in Lothian and Borders. One of these experienced a fourth interview in Lothian and Borders.

Table 9.9   Duration of second stage of investigation

Duration	% of cases
Under half hour	9
0.5.- 1 hour	22
1 - 2 hours	42
2 - 3 hours	13
3 - 4 hours	4
4 - 5 hours	6
Over 5 hours	4

9.8   PROVISION OF INFORMATION AND FURTHER CONTACT

In most Forces complainers are given a leaflet with details of the specialist officer's name and telephone number. This enables the complainer to convey additional information about the incident to the specialist officer. According to Officer 7,

> "Two or three days later sometimes people remember a bit better. We always give them our phone number and name. Sometimes they remember something more, and can phone up and say 'I just want to add something to my statement.'"

It will be recalled from Chapter 5 that the telephone numbers of specialist Units are not listed in any local telephone directories.

The amount of contact between specialist officers and complainers after the investigation is complete differs considerably from Force to Force. The type and frequency of contact is dependent on the officer's workload and geographical factors, with some officers staying in touch with complainers by telephone. Some officers regularly update women about progress in their case. Others are less methodical unless the woman contacts them. The SHHD guidelines (1985) emphasised the necessity for complainers to be kept informed of progress, particularly when it is decided not to refer the case to the Procurator Fiscal. In some Units, all correspondence for the women is sent to the specialist officer. All correspondence regarding citations and arrangements for precognitions is then forwarded to her. This preserves the anonymity of the complainer within her community and ensures that the specialist officer can discuss and clarify relevant procedural issues in confidence.

Officers do not see it as their role to offer support or advice to the complainer beyond the investigative stage, apart from providing information about the progress of the case. As Officer 8 put it,

"In almost every case we will have to go out and re-interview her again over the next day or so, usually the day after. This is for further information or clarification, especially if we trace somebody or other witnesses ..... perhaps to accompany her for an ID. We don't have a lot of contact with her beyond that, we see her as often as is needed to get the information, but we haven't got the resources to go back and see her again and again."

Over one third of officers said they would like to have more contact with complainers. According to Officer 8,

"Personally I would like to have more. I feel as if it just doesn't happen as much as it should, basically because of our workload. You'll go on to be dealing with something else the next day. You've already made that first important contact and that person might think that you are the only one they feel they can speak freely to, and that happens a lot. You might get them phoning you at the office and leaving messages, not wanting to speak to any of the other officers. You might find they will come into the office to see you if they can't get you on the phone. So I feel that it would be a good idea if we could be formally delegated where we should go and make an actual follow-up visit afterwards. A lot of times I will try and fit one in as best as I can and go out and see the person, but sometimes it just doesn't happen."

9.8.1 Information leaflets

Most Forces have devised leaflets for women who have been sexually assaulted. These are given to women at the end of the first stage of enquiries. They provide information about the enquiry process and specific procedures, facilities and follow-up interviews by police. Information and advice relating to pregnancy, sexually transmitted diseases and the Criminal Injuries Compensation Board is also given. Leaflets also give the name and contact number of the specialist officer, the name of the investigating/enquiry officer (CID), names and telephone numbers of medical clinics and space to note local resources offering support to women. Several Units also distribute information from local support and counselling agencies.

9.9 OUTCOME OF INVESTIGATION

Table 9.10 lists the outcome of police investigations in the 136 cases recorded for this study. In 55 of the 136 cases (40%) the suspect was apprehended by the police, charged, and a report was sent to the Procurator Fiscal.

Table 9.10   Outcome of police investigations

Force	Total No of cases	No of Rapes	Rapes				No. of assaults	Other Sexual Assaults*			
			Outcome					Outcome			
			Reported to PF	Unsolved	With-drawn	File only		Reported to PF	Unsolved	With-drawn	File only
Dumfries & Galloway	5	4	3	-	1	-	1	-	-	-	1
Grampian	11	6	3	-	2	1	5	3	-	-	2
Lothian & Borders	34	22	7	2	6	7	12	6	2	-	4
Northern	1	-	-	-	-	-	1	-	-	-	1
Strathclyde	65	29	13	5	6	5	36	11	7	2	16
Tayside	20	6	2	1	2	1	14	7	2	1	4

* Includes attempted rapes, assault with intent to ravish and indecent assault.

Nineteen of the cases (14%) were unsolved because the offender was not traced or the investigation was incomplete at the end of the data collection period.

Twenty of the cases (15%) were withdrawn by the complainer. These included twelve cases where the complainer retracted the allegations, stating that they were false. In three of these instances the complainer was charged with wasting police time. In eight cases the complainer decided not to proceed with the complaint. The main reason for this was not wanting to undergo a police investigation. The remaining 42 cases (31%) were not investigated by the police because of insufficient evidence, or because they were groundless or unfounded. It is not possible to indicate how many of these were not recorded or noted as "no-crime".

Of the 67 rapes reported to the police, 28 (41%) were reported to the Procurator Fiscal. Of the 69 cases involving other types of sexual assault, 27 (39%) were reported to the Procurator Fiscal.

9.10   CONCLUSION

Where a report of a serious sexual assault is made to the police, when it is made and how it is made are all factors which may affect the nature of the initial contact between the police and women reporting an assault. The role of uniformed officers appears to have diminished, although they do still have involvement in ascertaining brief details and remaining with complainers until the arrival of a specialist officer.

Specialist officers provide a continuous link with the complainer, reducing the number of times she has to repeat her account of what happened. They are also alert to the needs of women reporting sexual assault. In some Forces there is an emphasis on building trust to facilitate a smoother investigation and reduce the trauma for the complainer.   Specialist officers are less concerned with disproving an allegation of sexual asssault than officers interviewed in previous studies and they are also more concerned with the welfare of the complainer. Although some officers still hold sceptical attitudes these are not as widespread, nor as dogmatic as those found by Chambers and Millar (1983).

The inception of specialist Units has meant that fewer police officers are involved in investigations. Specialist officers function as a 'buffer' between the complainer and the investigating officer, reducing the amount of contact between them. Most communication between the complainer and investigating officer is now done via the specialist officer.

There have been improvements in the timing and location of medical examinations and a reduction in the number of examinations undergone by complainers. There is still room, however, for improvements in the working arrangements between police and police surgeons in some Forces.

Finally, interview suites provide a much better environment for the interview and medical examination of complainers. Several Forces appear to have adopted the idea of letting the women go home and rest after the first stage of the investigation and this can be seen as another area of improvement.

Footnotes

1   Dumfries and Galloway, Grampian, Lothian and Borders, Strathclyde and Tayside.
2   The possibility that some incidents are dealt with without being drawn to the attention of the specialist officer cannot be discounted. Several writers refer to the way in which some incidents brought to the attention of the police by women are dealt with in such a way that they do not proceed beyond the reporting stage. See, for example, McCabe, S & Sutcliffe, F. (1978) Defining Crime: A Study of Police Decision Making; Edwards, S. Policing Domestic Violence (1989); Chambers, G. and Millar, A. (1983) Investigating Sexual Assault.
3   In some Forces a monitoring system was set up by senior officers as a means of checking forms for accuracy and thoroughness. In other Units there was no such system. During fieldwork visits, several officers said they had not filled in forms due to pressure of work.
4   In nine cases, the initial classification of an incident recorded on the form was changed at a later stage of the investigation. For example, two incidents recorded as rape in Lothian and Borders were reclassified as clandestine injury, as was one case of rape in Strathclyde. Also in Strathclyde, three incidents initially recorded as rape were recorded to offences under s.106 or s.107 of the Mental Health (Scotland) Act 1984 as were rape incidents in Grampian and Lothian and Borders. In Dumfries and Galloway, the indecent assault was later recoded as attempted sodomy. This was the only case involving a male that was marked as an 'adult sexual assault'.
5   Amir, M (1971) Patterns in Forcible Rape, University of Chicago Press; Chambers, G. and Millar, A. (1983) Investigating Sexual Assault.
6   CC Circular 7/1985.
7   Chambers, G. and Millar, A. (1983) Chapter 8.
8   Ibid. See also Edwards, S (1989), Bourlet, A. (1990).
9   Details of the procedure of medical examinations are outlined in Chambers and Millar (1983) pp 102 - 107.
10   Ibid. p 99.

CHAPTER 10

WORKING RELATIONSHIPS WITH VOLUNTARY ORGANISATIONS

In this Chapter consideration is given to the working relationship between the police and local voluntary support agencies. It draws on information from the data collection exercise and from the postal questionnaire which was sent to voluntary support agencies throughout Scotland.

10.1 DEVELOPING CONTACT WITH SUPPORT AGENCIES

Chambers and Millar (1983) highlighted the importance of providing advice and information to complainers regarding local support and counselling agencies. They found that, in general, the police did not see this activity as part of their role and they were selective in the complainers they referred to other agencies. They found limited contact between the police and local support agencies.

The SHHD guidelines which followed the report recommended that a complainer 'should be told of any appropriate local services, whether medical, social, voluntary, which could be of assistance to her.'[1] They also recommended that 'details about Rape Crisis Centres and victim support schemes (where they exist) and the services they offer should, where appropriate, also be given.'

These recommendations were endorsed in several sets of Force instructions which explicitly stated that the Units and specialist officers had a role in providing this sort of advice and information to complainers. Some sets of instructions made Units responsible for developing and sustaining contact with outside statutory organisations such as the SWD, the Procurator Fiscal, the Reporter and local support agencies such as Rape Crisis Centres.

10.1.1 Support agencies

The number and range of support agencies which offer specialist advice and information for women who have been sexually assaulted varies across Scotland. Rape Crisis Centres (RCC) and Women's Aid groups are established in many Scottish cities. Other support agencies include Victim Support Schemes (VSS), Citizen's Advice Bureaux (CAB), Incest Survivor Groups and local support and/or counselling resources for women. In some areas, the RSSPCC offers counselling for women who have been sexually abused. There are also support groups specifically for black and Asian women in Edinburgh and Glasgow. In addition, local authority SWDs and housing departments, medical and sexually transmitted disease clinics also offer advice and information.

Postal questionnaires were sent to twenty seven support agencies across Scotland. These included RCCs, VSSs, Women's Aid groups, RSSPCC and local groups offering support, information and counselling for women who have been sexually assaulted. Information was sought on the amount and type of contact that existed between the support agencies and the specialist Units. Questionnaires were completed and returned by twenty two agencies, representing a response rate of 81%.

10.2   NATURE AND EXTENT OF CONTACT : VIEWS OF SUPPORT AGENCIES

10.2.1 How agency learnt of Unit

Table 10.1 shows how the agency learnt about the existence of the Unit in their area. Thirteen agencies reported that contact was initiated by the Unit, although the stage at which contact was made varied between agencies and areas. Only five agencies were informed when the Units were set up. Most agencies responded by requesting further information from the Units regarding their work. This was forthcoming in twelve cases, although the agencies concerned considered such information to be too brief or too limited.

Table 10.1   How agencies learnt about Unit

Source	Number
Written information sent by Unit	5
Verbally contacted by Unit	7
Talk/presentation by Unit	1
From women who had reported assault	3
Referral by Unit	3
Through the media	3

10.2.2 Agencies' involvement in setting up units

Three agencies had some involvement in the setting up of the local Unit. Two RCCs had an input into the first training courses for specialist officers and a RSSPCC office was involved in the discussion and planning stages of a specialist response with an emphasis on child abuse.

10.2.3 Impressions of Units

Representatives from seventeen agencies had visited their local Unit and/or interview suite. This was at the invitation of the police in six cases (4 VSS's, 1 RCC and 1 RSSPCC). In six further cases it was in response to a request by the agency. The remaining five visits to Units were made when an agency worker accompanied a woman during a police investigation.

Overall, respondents had a favourable impression of facilities in the interview suites. The suites were described as "sheltered and secure", "well-equipped", and "designed to minimise discomfort". Criticisms were that the facilities were "too clinical" and, in a few cases "difficult to access" because they had no separate entrance, were upstairs, or were reached by walking through the police building.

The attitudes and approach of individual specialist officers were also viewed positively by support agencies. The majority of officers were described as "helpful", "considerate", "sympathetic" and "interested", with only a minority described as "unsympathetic" or "disaffected".

10.2.4 Type of contact

Three agencies said they never came into contact with Units, fifteen said their contact was infrequent and four said that they were often in contact with the Unit. Three of the latter agencies were victim support schemes. Eight agencies which had frequent contact dealt with one specific officer. These were not always specialist officers, but rather a particular 'contact' officer in the Force. In Strathclyde, three agencies had positive contact with an officer responsible for training specialist officers, although they had little contact with officers in the Units.

Table 10.2   Contact between Units and other agencies

Nature of contact	Number of agencies
Referrals from Unit	10
Referrals to Unit	10
Talks/presentations to Unit	7
Talks/presentations by Unit	3
Accompanying women to Unit	15
Training input	3
Requests to Unit for information/advice	3

Note: some agencies have more than one type of contact.

10.2.5 Agency information available in the Units

Thirteen agencies reported that Units gave out information on the service they provided to women who had been assaulted. All understood this to consist of a contact telephone number and brief information regarding the service. Two agencies said that Units did not carry any information regarding their services and the remaining seven agencies did not know if Units gave out information about them. All the agencies in the sample wanted Units to carry more information on local support services. Suggestions included wallposters, advice sheets and information packs. Two agencies reported sending large quantities of information packs to Units but said that these packs were not distributed to complainers.

10.2.6 Quality of relationship

The majority of agencies (18) felt that the quality of the relationship they had with the Units was "good", "positive" or "reasonable" and in two cases it was reported to be "excellent". They also said, however, that the contact was limited. The remaining four agencies were critical of the quality of the relationship, describing it as "poor" or "very poor." The reasons cited for this included "very difficult to make contact with specialist officers" (particularly in Strathclyde where, in most Units, only one officer is on duty per shift), "general resistance by police to [agency's] perspective on violence against women", and the "unhelpful and intimidating" stance taken by police to the services offered by the agency.

Several agencies also mentioned the way in which staff changes could affect the quality of their relationship with the Unit. Agencies were never informed of the changeover, and contact and relationships had to be re-established after each change of staff.

10.3   CONCLUSION

On the whole, local support agencies saw specialist Units as a considerable improvement on prior police practice in the investigation of sexual assault. Interview suites were seen as a specific improvement, providing privacy, security and more comfortable and amenable surroundings for the interviewing and medical examination of complainers. Another important factor was the availability of trained and informed female officers to provide continuity on a one-to-one basis with complainers throughout the investigation. Several agencies stated that the

Units provided a more sympathetic and sensitive police response to sexual assault. The attitude of specialist officers was believed to be sensitive and more understanding of the experience of violence towards women.

Some support agencies also saw disadvantages in the specialist Units. These included a lack of change in the rest of the Force because they perceived that something was being done; restricted skill development by male officers because the work is done predominantly by women officers; "ghettoising" of female officers and the consequent marginalisation of work involving violence against women. The use of untrained uniformed officers when specialist officers were unavailable was also seen as a disadvantage. One agency referred to the Units as a "token gesture with no overall change in policy or practice." Other disadvantages concerned the way in which officers were selected for the work. It was felt that this did not guarantee a sensitive approach and created the potential for resentment among officers who felt they had to do such work.

Footnote

---

1   CC Circular 7/1985

CHAPTER 11

THE INVESTIGATION OF CHILD ABUSE

This Chapter describes the joint working arrangements which exist between Units and regional SWDs for the investigation of child abuse. It also documents the procedures which are implemented following a report of suspected abuse. The information is based on individual Force and regional social work policy documents, material from interviews with police officers and social workers and from the data collection exercise.

11.1 JOINT WORKING

11.1.1 A dynamic area

Discussions between police and social workers on investigative arrangements for child abuse were taking place in all Forces throughout the period of the research. The aim in all areas was to establish formal joint procedures to be followed in most cases of child abuse. In other parts of Britain, joint investigative arrangements have focused on child sexual abuse. In Scotland, however, the aim has been to devise joint codes of practice which are applicable in cases of suspected physical and sexual abuse and in several Forces these have extended to child neglect.

This is an area of work which is characterised by continual developments on a range of issues including notification procedures, information sharing, joint interviews and training and the incorporation of joint procedures into formal policy. Some developments have taken place at a local level and practice can vary within a region.

11.1.2 Difficulties with classification

Research describing police/social work practice in the investigation of child sexual abuse has identified difficulties in categorising joint investigative arrangements[1] and broad categorisations can misrepresent or obscure local practice. One approach has been to devise a system which is flexible enough to represent the different stages of the investigation and other activities which characterise local responses to child abuse.

The classification devised by Moran-Ellis et al (1991) is particularly useful. Concepts of 'joint' and 'separate' are placed at opposite ends of an investigative continuum, with 'degrees of jointness' identified at various points. All components of the investigation can be accommodated on a scale against which the points and types of inter-agency contact can be plotted. Three distinct types of joint approach were identified:

- separate
- informal joint
- formal joint

The distinction between the latter types is dependent on the extent to which procedures are written into police Force Orders and social work practice guidelines or instruction manuals.[2]

11.1.3 'Degrees of jointness' in investigations

It is possible to apply this model to specialist Units in Scotland. Police and social workers in all regions assert that child abuse investigations are carried out with reference to the other agency at some stage of the proceedings. There are, however, differences in the extent to which specific aspects of the investigation are carried out jointly and the procedures articulated in agency guidelines. An example of a 'formalised joint approach' is the CPU in Fife. Police and social workers are based in the Unit and a joint approach is stipulated in all aspects of their work from receipt of a report of suspected child abuse to the final outcome of the investigation. A joint strategy is agreed for interviewing all witnesses including the child and a joint report is presented to the initial case conference. Interviewing of a suspect remains a duty for the police alone and the CPU social workers have minimal involvement with a case after the investigation stage.

A similar arrangement exists in Central CPU, although police and social workers are not based in the same office. Instead, specialist child protection social workers are based in local social work area offices. When a referral of suspected abuse is made to either agency the other is informed, a strategy meeting is held and joint interviews are undertaken. The social worker allocated to the case may conduct any follow-up work with the child and this has implications for that worker's availability for investigating any subsequent new cases. In Northern, the police Child Abuse Co-ordinator acts as a centralised resource receiving new referrals, contacting social workers if they are not the source of the referral and allocating a police officer to the case. Before an investigation commences, the Co-ordinator and relevant social work team leader assess if a joint approach is necessary. If it is, the designated police officer and social worker hold a meeting to share information and discuss the case. They interview the child and other witnesses jointly and they work together for the duration of the investigation. Instructions for all of these procedures are set out in Force Orders and social work department practice guidelines.

Dumfries and Galloway, Tayside and Grampian operate an 'informal joint approach'. Although there are no formal arrangements, joint investigation is the norm for specialist officers and social workers. Force Orders state the need to notify the social work department and undertake joint interviews of the child. They do not, however, refer to joint procedures in other aspects of the investigation. Social work guidelines or instructions refer to the need to notify the police in cases of suspected child abuse. Decisions to undertake joint investigations are usually taken by a senior social worker or team leader and the relevant DCI or Inspector. There are also local differences in practice within Forces.

In Lothian and Borders and Strathclyde the procedures for joint investigations are not written into Force Orders or social work guidelines/instructions. In both agencies, however, there are statements regarding the notification of suspected cases of abuse. Both agencies also encourage a co-ordinated and co-operative approach in child abuse investigations and there is considerable variation in local practice. In some areas there is a 'separate' approach with minimal contact between agencies. In others there is some inter-agency consultation on individual cases and there are areas where joint investigative interviews take place on an ad hoc basis. In other areas specialist police officers and local social workers work closely together, undertaking joint interviews with the child and other witnesses in every case.

11.1.4 Initial decisions on joint investigations

Not all allegations of child abuse are passed between agencies. The decision of social workers to notify the police is dependent on a number of factors. These include situations where a criminal offence may have been committed. Many social workers identified situations where this was not clear and they were unsure of the necessity for a joint approach. Another factor relates to the type and seriousness of the abuse. In general, it can be said that all referrals of suspected sexual abuse and serious physical abuse are notified to the Unit by social workers. Sometimes less serious cases of suspected physical abuse or neglect are not referred until some initial enquiries have been made by the social worker.

Another factor relates to the initial information which the social worker receives about a case. Anonymous phonecalls, or information that children have been left on their own are sometimes followed up on an informal basis by the social worker. In these cases an assessment of the situation is made by checking social work records for any previous contact with the family, discussing the allegation and making initial enquiries. At this stage the appropriateness of contacting the police is also assessed. Social workers feel that doing this preliminary work before contacting the police is advantageous to a joint investigation. As one social worker said,

"It becomes a joint investigation as soon as you pick up the phone and tell the police about it." (SW3/2).

The police were also able to identify situations where cases of abuse reported to them did not require social work involvement. Examples included abuse by a stranger, one-off flashers and under-age sex between two teenagers. In these cases specialist officers spoke of contacting social workers if they felt that counselling for the victim was appropriate.

Interviews with police and social workers in areas where there are no formal arrangements for conducting joint investigations revealed another important factor. Apprehension or unease about making a mistake in complex or serious cases was seen as a deterrent to conducting single-agency interviews by nine specialist police officers and eleven social workers. In these cases joint interviewing was seen as providing a safety net in a difficult situation. As one experienced social worker noted,

"Two different heads are always better than one in circumstances of indecision or doubt." (SW 7/3)

A specialist police officer echoed this view,

"Social workers are our safety net. For the ones that we don't have enough evidence for, they can take action to safeguard the child".(Officer 11)

11.2   REPORTS OF CHILD ABUSE: THE DATA

Specialist officers dealt with 710 reports of child abuse during the four month data collection period. Child abuse accounted for the majority of enquiries (79%) undertaken by specialist officers.

Table 11.1   Child abuse cases reported to Units

Force	Child abuse	Other cases	Total
Central	122	-	122
Fife CPU [1]	54	4	58
Dumfries and Galloway	22	5	27
Grampian	46	11	57
Lothian and Borders	155	36	191
Northern	30	3	33
Strathclyde	279	108	387
Tayside [2]	2	21	23
Total	710	188	898

1   At the time of this exercise, only one CPU was in operation in Fife, covering one police Division only.

2   In Tayside, the data collection form recorded cases of adult sexual assault. The two cases here refer to reports by adult survivors of abuse during childhood.

Table 11.1 shows that in Dumfries and Galloway, Grampian and Lothian and Borders, child abuse enquiries accounted for approximately 80% of the workload of the Units. In Northern, child abuse accounted for over 90% and in Strathcylde, the percentage was slightly lower at 72%. Although it was only possible to record cases of adult sexual assault in Tayside, officers estimated that only 70% to 80% of thier work related to child abuse enquiries. This reflects the figures in other Force areas.

11.2.1 Type of child abuse

Sixty three percent of child abuse cases were categorised by officers as sexual abuse, 27% as physical abuse and 6% as neglect. The remaining 4% involved a combination of all three categories of abuse.[3]

11.2.2 Victims of child abuse

Females accounted for 66% of referrals and males for 34%. Their age range is shown in Table 11.2.

Table 11.2   Age of children in child abuse investigations

Age	% in sample
0-1 year	6
1-5 years	21
5-10 years	28
10-12 years	19
12-16 years	26
Total	100

Less than 1% of enquiries involved children of Asian or Afro-Caribbean origin.

11.3 THE INVESTIGATIVE PROCESS

In this section, the main aspects of the investigative process are described. Interview material is used to illustrate differences and similarities in joint working practices throughout Scotland.

11.3.1 Notification of child abuse

The police are notified of cases of suspected abuse by members of the public and child protection agencies, particularly social workers. Police are concerned by unwarranted delays by social workers in informing them of cases, a point which has also been noted by other researchers.[4]

Specialist officers in dual-responsibility Units spoke of social workers "dragging their feet" and "taking their time" in notifying police. This delay, they felt, hampered the police in their duty to investigate and conflicted with a police objective to be involved "from the earliest possible stage." It has already been noted, however, that social workers can justify some of the delay in passing on information to the police.

Social workers thought that police sometimes tended to move too quickly once they were informed of a suspected child abuse case. As one summed up,

> "The police have fairly well-defined paths to tread in an investigation, and they want to storm down them immediately they think a crime may have been committed." (SW 3/2)

In at least 25% of the cases in this study, other professionals including social workers, doctors and teachers had interviewed the child before notifying the case to the police.

11.3.2 Source of referrals

Most referrals from other agencies were made by means of telephone calls to the Units. Where uniformed officers are notified of suspected cases, internal communication systems exist to ensure that Units are informed at the earliest possible stage. Table 11.3 shows the source of child abuse referrals made to the specialist Units.

Table 11.3   Source of referral for suspected child abuse cases

Source of referral	% of sample
Social Workers	44
Health professionals	8
Teachers	9
Parent/guardian	7
Other relatives [1]	6
Friends/neighbours	7
Anonymous phonecalls	3
Local police	4
Support agencies [2]	3
Victim	9
Total	100

1   Includes grandparents, aunts, uncles and older siblings.
2   Includes Childline

The majority of cases (44%) were referred to the Units by social workers. Family, friends and neighbours were the referral source in 20% of cases and doctors, nurses and teachers accounted for 17% of cases. Table 11.3 shows that 9% of cases were reported by the victim. Most of these were adult victims reporting past abuse from their childhood. All Forces reported an increase in the number of these referrals.

11.3.3   Time of referrals

Most reports (67%) were made to the police during weekday office hours. 23% of cases, however, were notified to the police at night or weekends. Most of these reports were from sources other than social work, although a small number came from social work Emergency Duty Teams (EDTs).

It has already been noted that the majority of specialist officers work a shift system and most social workers work a five day week with day-time office hours. This is an organisational issue which, according to both officers and social workers in the regions concerned, frequently leads to problems. When a referral which requires an emergency response is received by the police after office working hours, joint working is inhibited. It can also mean that an investigator begins the work with one professional counterpart, only to change at a later stage of the investigation.

11.3.4   Information exchange

The quality and range of information exchanged about a case at the outset of an investigation is important for deciding the subsequent course of action. This is particularly so if a joint investigation is planned. A common concern of police and social workers relates to differences in the quality and amount of information sought and exchanged between each professional.[5] This relates to occupational differences in perspective and professional requirements in the work. Police require "clear-cut information", "factual evidence" and " explicit information". Hard evidence cannot always be provided by social workers and police were often disparaging of social workers' time-consuming preoccupation with "what might be best for the family" and "looking deeper into the possible reasons for the alleged abuse." As Officer 2 summed up,

"We don't have the time to sit and analyse the family."

Social workers, on the other hand, were concerned at the police preoccupation with "facts", "evidence and prosecutions" and "criminal justice" which they felt had difficulty relating to social work concerns about the welfare of the child and the family.

11.3.5 Planning the investigation

Police and social workers agreed that information-sharing and consultation between agencies at an early stage clarified the need for a joint investigation. The majority of police and social workers emphasised that early consultation led to better quality planning in the initial stages of an investigation.

Where an emergency response is not required because there is no immediate risk to the child, police and social workers have an opportunity to plan the enquiry. There is now a much greater recognition of the value of dialogue and discussion to determine the most appropriate course of action. In a few areas, however, negative views about the usefulness of such early consultation remain entrenched.

11.3.6 Strategy meetings

If a joint interview is agreed, a 'strategy meeting' between the specialist officer and social worker allocated to the case takes place. Most of these meetings take place en route to the source of the referral. Both professionals exchange information collected from their respective record systems and a broad plan of action is formulated. A statement is then obtained from the source of the referral, after which the child is interviewed if this is felt to be appropriate.

11.4   INTERVIEWS WITH CHILDREN

Interviews with children were undertaken in 690 (97%) of cases dealt with by specialist officers. The main reasons for not interviewing children were when the child was too young, too distressed, where the referral was "malicious" or "too vague" or where initial enquiries indicated that an interview was not necessary. Table 11.4 shows the numbers of joint and police-only interviews undertaken with child victims.

Table 11.4   Types of interview undertaken

Force	Total	Joint interviews	Police- only interviews
Central CPU	116	93 (80)	23 (20)
Fife CPU	52	37 (71)	9 (17) *
Dumfries and Galloway	22	10 (45)	12 (55)
Grampian	44	26 (59)	18 (41)
Lothian and Borders	150	23 (15)	127 (85)
Northern	29	21 (72)	8 (28)
Strathclyde	275	49 (18)	226 (82)

Numbers in brackets refer to percentages.   * 6 cases (12%) were investigated by CPU social workers only.
In the two cases reported in Tayside, interviews were undertaken by police only.

Table 11.4 shows the variation between Forces in the type of interview undertaken and it reflects the extent to which formalised arrangements exist for joint interviews. The majority of victim interviews in Fife (71%), Central (80%) and Northern (79%) were conducted jointly; in Grampian over half (59%) were joint; in Dumfries and Galloway just under half (45%) were joint. Joint interviews were undertaken in fewer cases in Lothian and Borders (15%) and Strathclyde (18%). Both of these Forces and their corresponding SWDs are currently reviewing child abuse procedures, with the intention of implementing formalised joint arrangements.[6]

Local variations become obscured when each Force is examined as a whole. For example, there is wide variation in practice within Lothian and Borders, where one police Force works with two SWDs. Two Units in the Force undertook a significantly higher percentage of joint interviews than the other two Units, where joint interviews were rare. Similarly, in Strathclyde, three Units undertook no joint interviews and in another three Units almost two thirds of interviews were jointly undertaken.

In Fife, Central and Northern, joint interviews take place for all types of abuse, regardless of the seriousness of the allegation or the age of the child. In other Forces, however, joint interviews take place more often in cases of sexual abuse and serious physical abuse, particularly where a younger child is involved.

11.4.1 Taking the lead in interviews

Interviews with police and social workers indicate that it is generally the police who take the lead in joint interviews; they set the parameters of the interview and dictate the order of questions. Exceptions to this are the CPUs, where specialist officers are happy for social workers to take the lead. Indeed, police often rely on social workers' notes, such is the high level of trust and mutual respect that has built up. Here there is also greater flexibility concerning roles in the interview. This is attributed to social workers gaining an understanding of legal-evidential requirements and the role of the police. Social workers, on the other hand, attribute it to the establishment of a broader collaborative role with the police and the development of a "more consistent approach" in interviews.

In other regions, social workers are encouraged to "take a back seat" until the police have finished their interview. Thereafter, according to police, social workers "are free to ask whatever questions they wish for their own records."

11.4.2 Objectives of interviews with children

Waterhouse and Carnie (1990) noted the competing professional objectives which exist in joint investigations. [6] The interview with a child is often the single most important part of the investigation and it was identified by police and social workers in this research as the main site of professional conflict. Although both agencies share a concern with the welfare and interests of the child, their respective views concerning the function of the interview are not easily reconciled.

Police emphasised the primary purpose of interviews to elicit, without asking leading questions, information for legal-evidential purposes. Social workers see the investigative interview primarily as an evaluation of risk to the child and for deciding on a stategy for intervention.

11.4.3 The nature of interview questions

Professional perspectives can also affect the nature and quality of information sought in the interview. Approximately half of the specialist officers felt that social workers tend to ask leading or "irrelevant" questions, thus running the risk of contaminating evidence in joint interviews. Conversely, ten officers felt that social workers came to the interview with more experience in communicating with children than the police, and that conducting joint interviews was an important learning experience for them. Chapter 4 has already noted that, prior to the establishment of specialist Units, the police tended to treated female and child witnesses in a similar fashion, interviewing children in the same way as adults. Observing the skills social workers use to communicate with children was an illuminating experience for many officers. One experienced police officer pointed out,

> "I would have run out of ideas and techniques after ten minutes [with the child]. If I wasn't able to get the child to speak after ten minutes, my powers of imagination didnae let me proceed. In the first interviews I would let the social worker take over and I would just listen, and pick up tips from them. I was learning from them." (Officer 10)

Some social workers said that they found it a considerable strain to conduct interviews jointly with the police. Twelve felt that police require more training in interviewing and communicating with children. They described police interviewing techniques as "heavy-handed", "inflexible" "unimaginative", and sometimes even "potentially frightening for the child." They also felt that the police sometimes used inappropriate techniques, such as playing 'name the body part' games with teenagers when these games were designed for use with much younger children. According to one social worker,

> "It's like you can teach the police techniques and games to get children to relax and speak, but they apply them in a totally inappriopriate way." (SW 7/1)

Furthermore, most social workers felt that the police did not respond positively to constructive criticism, so interviewing techniques remained a source of conflict. Some stated that they had to spend time after the police had finished questioning, in "normalising" the situation with the child.

Another contentious area concerns cases where police insist that the parents of a child are not informed about the interview because they are suspects. Social workers had strong misapprehensions about this and thought that differences of opinion between police and social workers on informing parents reflected a fundamental difference in perspective. In this situation police concern with obtaining "uncontaminated" evidence contrasts with the social work concern with family dynamics. As one social worker pointed out,

> "We are left having to turn up [to the parents] and say 'the police have spoken to your child at school, and the doctor did an examination and says this ....' It's very difficult for us in those circumstances." (SW 3/3)

11.4.4 Presence of others during interviews

In general, neither police or social workers like non-professional people to be present during the interview, although this depends on the needs of the child.

11.4.5 Site of child victim interviews

Table 11.5 shows where interviews with children took place.

Table 11.5   Site of first interview

Force	Hospital/ surgery	Interview suite	Victim's home	Other Home*	Other School	Other**
Central	2	19	65	17	6	7
Fife	-	8	19	2	14	9
Dumfries & Galloway	1	3	14	1	2	1
Grampian	1	12	26	-	2	3
Lothian & Borders	10	20	81	17	8	14
Northern	1	9	12	-	2	5
Strathclyde	13	93	123	24	7	15
Tayside	-	2	-	-	-	-
Total	28(5)	166(24)	340(49)	61(8)	41(6)	54(8)

Figures in brackets represent percentages
* home of relative, friend or neighbour
** includes police offices, sw offices, scout camp, activity camps, List D residential schools

Almost half the interviews (49%) were undertaken in the child's home and a quarter (24%) took place in a Unit interview suite. The majority of police and social workers felt that the child's home was often the most appropriate place to interview, provided there was a degree of privacy and the abuse had not occurred there.

11.4.6 Facilities for children with special needs

Six per cent of children in the data sample were identified by police as having "special needs" which made communication difficult. These included sight, hearing or speech impairment, learning difficulties, epilepsy or language difficulties. Officers reported difficulties in conducting interviews in these cases, because police had limited access to specialist services, apart from a signer for the deaf in some Forces.

11.4.7 Duration of child victim interviews

Police and social workers noted that the duration of an interview is dependent on a range of factors, including the child's age and their level of language development. The child's willingness to speak, the nature and circumstances of the case and the experience of the interviewers in eliciting information from children are also important. Table 11.6 shows the length of time taken for first interviews, indicating that there is little difference in length for a joint or a police-only interview.

Table 11.6   Duration of first interview

Duration of interview	Joint interviews	Police-only interviews
	%	%
0 - 0.5 hours	15	11
0.5 - 1 hour	30	34
1 - 2 hours	37	41
2 - 3 hours	11	12
3 - 4 hours	5	2
over 4 hours	2	-

Interviews with police and social workers revealed that where longer interviews take place, children are not questioned continuously. In these cases the interview time includes observation of the child and play-time.

11.4.8 Second interviews

Most children were interviewed only once but in 28% of cases (193) more than one interview was conducted. Most of these cases were suspected sexual abuse.   In 52 cases (79%) a total of two interviews were conducted. In 23 cases (12%) there were three interviews and in 18 cases (9%) there were four interviews.

When a joint first interview led to a second interview, two thirds of these were undertaken jointly; one third were carried out by police only. Second and subsequent interviews were much shorter than first interviews and none took longer than two hours. Specialist officers revealed that subsequent interviews, which they prefer to call "wee chats", are on points of clarification, rarely involving lengthy questioning of the child.

The importance of the child dictating the pace and the style of the interview was often stated by both police and social workers . A second interview is sometimes seen to be in the child's best interests, particularly in cases where they are young or have limited vocabulary.   Investigators also pointed out that disclosures of sexual abuse could take a considerable amount of time and they were more likely to occur after a level of trust has built up between the child and the interviewer. This normally takes more than one interview.

11.5   MEDICAL EXAMINATIONS

Police and social workers noted the difficulty of making decisions on medical examinations for children, particularly in cases of suspected sexual abuse. From the police perspective, medical examinations may yield important forensic evidence. Yet specialist officers are reluctant to subject the child to a speculative examination, which the majority consider intrusive and unpleasant, when the chances of such an examination producing evidence consistent with abuse are quite slim. Unless there is physical evidence of penetration, tissue damage or the presence of semen, medical examinations may not produce any corroborative evidence.

The majority of officers and social workers said that the most important consideration affecting the decision to examine hinges on what the child says concerning what happened. Social workers hoped the medical examination would provide objective confirmation of their subjective belief in what the child had told them. Police looked to the examination to provide corroborative medico-forensic evidence. A small number from both agencies said that they would organise a medical examination "to be on the safe side", particularly in allegations of sexual abuse.

In joint investigations, a joint decision is taken on the necessity of an examination, although specialist officers said that where there are disagreements, they retain "the casting vote." Medical examinations are organised and attended by specialist officers. In joint investigations they are also attended by social workers. Permission to examine has to be obtained from parents or guardians, and in the majority of medical examinations (78%) a parent, guardian, or other relative was present.

Medical examinations were carried out in 42% of child abuse cases (299), as shown in Table 11.7.

Table 11.7 Medical examinations in child abuse cases

Force	Total cases	One medical examination	Two medical examinations	Three medical examinations
Central	122	50	4	-
Fife	54	14	2	-
Dumfries and Galloway	22	5	-	-
Grampian	46	16	3	-
Lothian and Borders	155	48	11	-
Northern	30	14	3	-
Strathclyde	279	111	15	3
Tayside	2	-	-	-
Total	710	258	38	3

In 258 cases (36%) one medical examination took place; in 38 cases (5.3%) there was a second medical examination and in only three cases (0.4%) was there a third examination.

Medical examinations took place in a hospital, health centre, a doctor's surgery, or in the medical examination room of police interview suites. In Central, approximately one third of medical examinations took place in the child's home. All of these were in cases of suspected physical abuse. Central CPU officers hold the view that the child's home is the most appropriate place for examinations, providing it is clean, well-lit and the entire family is not present. It does not take place in the child's home if that is the site of the alleged abuse.

As already discussed in Chapter 9, different arrangements with police surgeons exist in each Force, and several Forces expressed dissatisfaction with current arrangements. Unless the abuse is reported shortly after it occurred there is usually not the same level of urgency to examine the child as there is in cases of adult sexual assault. 'Medical examination appointments' are usually made in advance by specialist officers. In general, examinations for suspected physical abuse are jointly undertaken by a police surgeon and a paediatrician, hospital doctor or a GP. In less serious cases of physical abuse, the examination may take place without the police surgeon, which can make it easier to organise. In cases of suspected sexual assault, the examination is undertaken by the police surgeon and a paediatrician - or in the case of an older girl, by a police surgeon and a gynaecologist.

As in medical examinations in adult sexual assault cases, the specialist officer is responsible for the collection and bagging of material evidence from the medical examination.

11.6 INTERVIEWS WITH OTHER WITNESSES

Although child abuse is rarely witnessed by other people, investigations usually include interviews with members of the child's family. Interviews may also take place with children who are friends of the victim. In joint investigations, interviews with other children and (non-abusing) parents tend to be undertaken jointly. In Central, the majority of all interviews, including those with teachers, neighbours and family friends are conducted jointly. In other Force areas these interviews are reported to be conducted by police only.

11.7 THE CASE CONFERENCE

The end of the investigation is frequently marked by the case conference, although there are different arrangements between regions for the timing of this. Different criteria are also used to call case conferences. In most Forces, attendance at case conferences is the duty of the specialist officer investigating the case, although sometimes attendance is by another, senior officer (usually from Community Involvement Branch), who acts as police representative. In Central, the specialist officer attends the initial case conference as a matter of course. Subsequent review case conferences are not routinely attended by them.

11.8 FURTHER CONTACT WITH CHILD

Specialist officers revealed that they spend little further time time in contact with the child after the completion of the investigation. A small number of officers, however, said that in the event of a trial, they escort the child to court in advance to show him or her around. In general, they felt hard-pressed for time and, as in the case of adult complainers, they did not spend as much time with the child victim in the post-investigation phase as some of them would have liked.

After-care of the child victim is seen as the domain of the SWD. Most specialist officers said they expect social workers to provide the child's family with information about the progress of the case, although if they are contacted by a family member they would pass on any available information.

11.9 OUTCOME OF CHILD ABUSE INVESTIGATIONS

In at least 44% of cases, a report was sent to the Procurator Fiscal (20% to Procurator Fiscal only and 24% to Procurator Fiscal and Reporter). There was some confusion regarding the status of the 'File' and 'Other' categories on the SPU/1 form, and it is possible in the returned forms they included reports which were sent to the Procurator Fiscal. Not all investigations were complete at the end of the data collection period; incomplete cases are listed under 'Other' on the SPU/1 form.

Table 11.8   Outcome of child abuse investigations

Force	PF	Reporter	PF and Reporter	SW	File	Other
Central	13	41	38	-	19	11
Fife	16	18	2	-	17	1
Dumfries and Galloway	10	2	1	1	6	2
Grampian	4	12	10	3	13	4
Lothian and Borders	47	33	18	17	22	18
Northern	11	8	3	-	6	2
Strathclyde	40	105	95	1	31	7
Tayside	2	-	-	-	-	-
TOTAL	143(20)	219(31)	167(24)	22(3)	114(16)	45(6)

Figures in brackets represent percentages.

11.10   POLICE TIME SPENT ON CHILD ABUSE INVESTIGATIONS

Specialist officers were asked to record the amount of time they spent on each enquiry. This included not only the investigation itself, but also time spent liaising with social workers and other agencies, attendance at case conferences and other tasks such as report writing and essential paperwork.   The length of time taken up in enquiries varies considerably from one case to another. They tend to be more time-consuming and span a longer period than other sorts of enquiries. This is for two reasons: firstly, specialist officers undertake the entire investigation; secondly, many investigations entail a large number of interviews including the child, siblings, parents, friends, teachers and other relatives.   There is little difference in the length of time spent on an investigation whether it is joint or police-only.

All specialist officers said that child abuse investigations constitute the major part of their workload and that time spent on child abuse enquiries is increasing dramatically.

Table 11.9 shows the time taken to complete child abuse enquiries. In 35% of cases the length of the investigation was between three and six hours. In 22% of cases it took between six and ten hours to complete and, as the Table shows, several cases took substantially longer.

Table 11.9   Time taken to complete police enquiries in child abuse investigations (hours)

Force	Less than 1/2 hour	1/2 - 1	1 - 3	3 - 6	6 - 10	10 - 15	15 - 20	20 - 24	24 - 48	48 - 72	72 - 96	96 - 120	120 - 200	Over 200	Incomplete enquiries*
Central		3	16	48	38	10	2								5
Dumfries and Galloway		1	4	7	9	1									-
Fife		2	11	22	9	1	5	1	1			1			1
Grampian			8	18	9	7	3		1						-
Lothian and Borders		2	27	36	28	12	18	8	3			1	9	3	8
Northern		1	4	9	5	3	3		1						4
Strathclyde	1	8	66	93	45	12	12	8	8	1	1	1		2	21
Tayside					2										-

* Enquiry incomplete at the end of data collection period.

96

11.11 ADVANTAGES AND PROBLEMS OF JOINT WORKING

In police and social work interviews, respondents were asked what they considered to be the advantages of joint investigations and what they considered to be impediments to them.

11.11.1 Advantages of joint working

On the whole, police and social workers had similar views on the main advantages of joint working, although it should be noted that police and social workers in the CPUs were much more positive about joint working than officers in areas with less formalised arrangements. Joint working was seen as advantageous in the following ways:

(i) **A child-centered approach** : both sets of investigators felt that the major beneficiary of joint working arrangements was the child. Joint interviews mean less interviews by both agencies. Police in particular felt that their approach was much more child-centred as a result of working alongside social workers.

(ii) **Improved communication** : it was felt that joint working had led to considerable improvements in inter-professional communication. In areas where some form of joint working exists, communication between agencies was now on personal level. The existence of the Units and more open lines of communication meant that social workers knew who to notify about a case. Improved communication also facilitated better co-ordination regarding the investigation of cases. Working relations between police and social workers were perceived to have improved considerably since the inception of the Units.

(iii) **More information** : police pointed to the advantages of obtaining full background information about a family to help in making decisions. Social workers felt that the advantages lay in being able to find out more information about the progress of cases which involve a criminal prosecution.

(iv) **Better planning** : both police and social workers felt that access to information meant that investigations could be better planned. Working out a strategy, however brief, in advance led to a more streamlined investigation. It also meant that there was less chance of overlap and repetition in the work and that there was more consistency in the approach to investigations.

(v) **Pooling of expertise** : both sets of investigators felt that they brought specific skills, knowledge and experience to each investigation. Social workers in particular felt that there were advantages in combining professional roles in a single investigation.

(vi) **Learning experience** : police identified skill enhancement and learning about communicating with children from social workers. Social workers felt they had learned more about the intricacies of the criminal justice system from their police counterparts.

(vii) **Increased trust and confidence** : the building up of confidence and trust was seen as an important by-product of successful joint working. Social workers felt that some police now showed less rigid views as a direct result of joint working.

(viii) **Mutual support and sharing of responsibility :** both police and social workers felt that joint working provided an opportunity for mutual support. This was particularly the case in rural areas where specialist officers often work alone. Investigating child abuse can be demanding and stressful work; both police and social workers felt that being able to talk about a case with someone who knew as much about it was a major advantage.

(ix) **Saving of staff time :** Joint working meant that each agency allocated one staff member instead of two for undertaking interviews.

11.11.2 Impediments to joint working

In general, CPU staff tended to play down difficulties they encountered in joint working. Investigators in other Forces were more vocal in identifying difficulties of joint working. These main areas were identified:

(i) **Organisational issues :** several sets of difficulties were identified in this respect. They include working hours, different areas of jurisdiction, officers working with a number of different social workers simultaneously and lack of resources, particularly in Units where officers have to juggle priorities in child abuse and sexual assault cases. Finally, where the police are specialised and social workers are generic, this can mean that officers do not investigate with the same social worker more than once, so there is little opportunity to build up a good working relationship.

(ii) **Professional roles and perspectives :** another set of difficulties relates to the perceived incompatibility of professional roles. Stereotypical perceptions of each professional group still prevail and in some Forces they are entrenched. Different approaches in investigations by police and social workers has also led to conflict.

Both agencies fear that involvement by the other could hinder their professional duties in an investigation. In interviews with children, social workers feel that police are often insensitive to the needs and welfare of the child. Police, on the other hand, are concerned with social workers asking leading questions in interviews. They also voiced concern about social workers' contamination of evidence by speaking to the perpetrator or members of the child's family about the abuse.

Both sets of investigators fear that joint investigations may create confusion for the child and the child's family about what is happening. The balance of power in investigations also remains an area of complexity and concern.

Social workers felt that the police have a specific interest in a case for particular purposes and for a short period of time, whereas they are involved on a more long-term basis. Some feel that their asssociation with the police in the investigative stage could potentially damage their professional relationships with clients in after-care work.

Legal processes could also hinder social work involvement in a case, particularly when this might involve working with the perpetrator. Three social workers reported being told by the Procurator Fiscal at case conferences that because the case was 'sub judice' they were prohibited from discussing with the perpetrator his interpretation of his behaviour.

(iii)   **Deskilling** : both sets of investigators felt that their professional identity could become eroded over time. Social workers reported being thought of as "police aides" who assist in criminal investigations. Police spoke of being called "glorified social workers" by their colleagues.

11.12   <u>CONCLUSION</u>

The investigation of child abuse has brought the police into a clearer working relationship with social workers and other professionals. The extent and degree of joint working is dependent on a range of factors, some of which relate to the organisational context in which the investigation takes place; others relate to the stage of development reached on joint working in individual Forces.

The inception of the Units has signalled an increase in knowledge between social work and the police about their respective roles, practice, organisational constraints and statutory responsibilities in child abuse investigations. Professional conflict, especially in relation to the timing and direction of an interview with a child is evident, but there have been improvements in the amount of information shared between the two agencies. Both agencies acknowledge that early consultation between police and social workers on individual cases leads to better quality planning for subsequent work.

Most children are now interviewed only once, and there have been improvements in the way in which these interviews are conducted by the police. Although the police tend to take the lead, in the CPUs responsibility for the interview's direction and content is shared more evenly. Interviews are now more 'victim-centred' and specialist officers have learnt more about appropriate interview techniques from their social work counterparts.
The decision to undertake a medical examination is taken on the basis of what a child has disclosed. Specialist officers acknowledge the unpleasantness of the process for children, especially when a medical may not provide corroborative evidence of abuse Both social workers and specialist officers identified a number of advantages and impediments to joint working. Advantages clearly point to improvements in communication between agencies, better and more co-ordinated planning for the investigation, the sharing of complementary skills and an increase in trust and support between both agencies. All of these developments contribute to lessening the ordeal of an investigation for the child victim. Organisational and professional role differences are the most obvious impediments to joint working.

Footnotes

---

1   Waterhouse, L and Carnie J. (1990) Child Sexual Abuse : The Professional Challenge; Conroy, S, Fielding,N and Tunstill, J (1990) Investigating Child Sexual Abuse; the Study of a Joint Initiative.

2   Moran-Ellis, J, Conroy, S, Fielding, N and Tunstill, J (1991) Investigation of Child Sexual Abuse: An Executive Summary.

3   The research recognises that the figure reported for sexual abuse reported here is high. It contrasts markedly with the number of cases reported on child abuse registers compiled by SWDs, which record a higher incidence of physical abuse. The figures are not, however, directly comparable.

4   Waterhouse, L. and Carnie, J. (1990); Brown, L. and Fuller, R.(1991) Joint Police/Social Work Investigation in Child Protection: A Study of Central Region's Joint Initiative.

5   Also noted by Waterhouse and Carnie (1990).

6   Since completion of the research, police and social work departments in Lothian and Borders have issued a new code of practice and guidance for joint investigation of child abuse.

CHAPTER 12

THE VIEWS OF SPECIALIST OFFICERS

This Chapter gives the views of specialist officers about the nature of their work and the role of the Units. It draws extensively on interview material with the officers, noting their comments in a number of areas including their approach to the work, the advantages and limitations of working in the Units, the more and less enjoyable aspects of the work and the stress generated by it.

12.1   GENERAL APPROACH TO THE WORK

Most officers thought that dealing with sexual crimes and child abuse warranted a "different approach" to other crimes and offences, even those where victims were involved. This was due to the "intimate nature" of sexual crimes; the "potential for trauma" that they involve; having to relate "highly distressing" details and having to speak about "deeply personal information." As Officer 2 said,

> "It's a much more in-depth and intimate thing [to be sexually assaulted]. It's not like somebody saying 'I was hit' or 'My house got broken into', no matter how upset they are about it. Sexual assault is different."

Taking a "different approach" did not mean, however, that investigative standards were affected in any way. As Officer 4 pointed out, in sexual assault cases legal-evidential criteria are,

> "... if anything, even more strict. You have that in the back of your mind in an investigation, you know, will this stand up in court ? You know from experience that there has to be very strong corroborated evidence. It makes you even more meticulous."

On the whole, officers from dual-responsibility Units felt that, despite some similarities, sexual assault and child abuse were quite different sorts of offences, each requiring a different approach by the police. When asked to state what they saw as the main similarities, officers referred to three aspects; the intimate nature of both types of crimes, the trauma for the victim and the fact that perpetrators were predominantly males who were known to the victims.

Officers identified several differences between working on sexual assault and child abuse cases. Firstly, joint working with social workers meant that child abuse investigations were undertaken in a different organisational context to the sexual assault of adults. Inter-agency communication and co-operation were required and child abuse investigations entailed having to satisfy these requirements, as well as pursuing a criminal investigation. Secondly, the emphasis on the protection of the child, meant that officers were also involved in deciding whether to remove the child from the home. This involves entirely different sorts of considerations to sexual assault cases, in which the gathering of evidence takes precedence over other factors. Thirdly, it was felt that different sets of skills were needed for communicating with children. As one officer pointed out,

"You approach a child in a completely different way to what you would an adult. They don't have the same language abilities for a start. You go prepared to crawl around on the floor. You probably need much more patience."

12.1.1 Balancing priorities

Officers in dual-responsibility Units thought that their work in child abuse and sexual assault cases was of equal importance. Several spoke of having to "balance priorities" when working simultaneously on both types of investigations. Although each individual case is decided upon its own merits, reports are informally prioritised in terms of whether an emergency response is needed. The volume of work in most Units means that prioritisation can be very difficult.

12.1.2 Investigative v support function

All but one officer stressed that, although their role as specialist officers incorporated a duty to offer support and care to victims, this did not overshadow what they saw as their main function, the gathering of evidence. They were police officers first and foremost, with a secondary role of giving care and support. As Officer 10 pointed out,

> "We are not that different to other investigating officers. The difference is we've been trained in such a manner that when we are investigating we do it with more tact, sympathy and understanding. So .... it is a support role that we do far more than other officers, but we are still investigating officers."

Officers were careful to point out, however, that their investigative and support functions were closely inter-linked. Several officers referred to the first meeting with a victim as being crucially important for establishing relations which would have an effect on the ensuing investigation. They were strongly of the opinion that if they could build some form of rapport and trust to ensure that the victim felt that they were being supported, then this would enhance the investigation and ultimately make their work easier. All officers stressed that co-operation from the victim greatly assisted the investigation.

12.2 VIEWS ON THE ADVANTAGES OF UNITS AND SPECIALIST OFFICERS

All officers felt that specialist Units represented an improvement in police practice, particularly in the area of sexual assault. The main improvement was seen to be in terms of what one officer called the "victim-centredness" of the investigation and several said that this meant that the investigation should proceed at "the victim's own pace", rather than "sacrificing what she felt and getting the statement as soon as possible." All officers felt that the Units had considerably lessened the trauma of reporting a sexual assault to the police.

Another advantage related to contact between the victim and one trained officer and the personal nature of that contact. As Officer 11 related ,

> "Before, the victim would be dealing with a police number. Whereas with us it is on first name terms. They know that they can get in touch with us any time that they like and that there is much more contact."

The environment provided by the interview suites and medical examination rooms was also seen as a distinct improvement. Officer 6 was not speaking entirely in jest when she graphically stated,

> "It's not the situation anymore that you have just a table, a chair and a bar of carbolic soap."

Officers felt that the specialist approach meant that investigations were more thorough, smoother, efficient and resulted in better quality evidence, due primarily to victim co-operation.

"I would like to think that we work well and efficiently here. We have built up a lot of experience. And it helps victims, they can sense it I am sure. Things get done a lot more efficiently, we do things properly the first time. And I would like to think that benefits the victims." (Officer 10)

12.3 ENJOYABLE ASPECTS OF THE WORK

12.3.1 Heightened responsibility

Not all specialist officers enjoyed their work in the Units (see 12.4 below). Several were resistant to becoming specialist officers and they were unable to avoid secondment. Despite this, most officers conceded that there were some positive aspects to the work. Most notably, rewards were associated with having heightened responsibility in investigations. As Officer 10 related,

"You get responsibility and decision-making which you don't get in uniform. When in uniform you do an enquiry and as long as the i's are dotted and the t's are crossed, it's okay. You don't have the time or the opportunity to be doing such a thorough investigation. If we want we can chap doors, we can chap the whole street up and ask 'Have you seen this child with a bruise?' But if you are in uniform you dinnae have the time or the chance. In the end it's going to be taken out of your hands by CID if it's serious.... you are not given that responsibility yourself. Whereas we do, we can take any decision we like - we can be as thorough or as unthorough as we like and it's down to your own personal pride if you want to do your work properly."

In the Units, unlike on the beat, officers have the opportunity to plan a strategy and make decisions about a course of action in investigations of serious crime. As Officer 16 pointed out,

"The more serious the case is, the more satisfying the work is, if we can reach a conclusion. We prove it, we charge and we report it."

Some officers thought that there could be some difficulties adjusting to uniform work after secondment.

"The most difficult thing will be adjusting back to uniform work. And adjusting to a shift and a rank structure again and having to report everything to a Sergeant. And having to act under his instructions all the time. Whereas in here, you are much more of a free agent." (Officer 5)

12.3.2 Continued involvement

Prior to secondment, officers undertook only certain aspects of an investigation. Working in the Units meant that they were able to "see the investigation right through" from beginning to end and this was seen as a positive and satisfying aspect of the work.

12.3.3 Teamwork

Working as part of a team was also described as enjoyable. Given the nature of some of the enquiries, officers felt that there were distinct advantages to working alongside other officers. In several Units there were strong feelings of solidarity amongst officers. As Officer 1 related,

> "There is a lot of discussion between ourselves. Sitting having a coffee, we can tell one another about our cases. There is nothing broken in terms of confidentiality. We are in the same boat, and it does help having others around."

12.3.4 Relationships with other professionals

Another enjoyable and rewarding aspect concerned the development of close professional relations with Procurator Fiscals, Reporters and, in some cases, with police surgeons and paediatricians. Officers related having more direct contact with these professionals since secondment to the Units. According to Officer 2,

> "Before the Unit, we had to ask a Sergeant to telephone the Fiscal and the Reporter for us. We weren't allowed to as uniform officers. Now we call them up direct and they call us direct."

Not only does this practice save time, but such rapport means that officers can usefully discuss cases and investigations with Reporters and Fiscals.

12.3.5 A valuable learning experience

Two-thirds of officers felt that working in the Units was a valuable working experience, and one that would stand them in good stead in their police career.

> " I've learnt more in here in six months than I learnt in six years in uniform."
>
> (Officer 1)

> " I feel much more experienced. I feel much more confident when dealing with people. The investigating experience has made me much more thorough in my work." (Officer 2)

> "I'd say it's made me a better police officer. I think I'm more aware of peoples' problems. When you are on the beat you tend to think of everyone as a criminal or a hoodlum. I've learnt to take a backward step in here. I can see the wider picture. It's done me good as an investigator, as an officer dealing with the public and as a person. It's done me a lot of good."(Officer 5).

A common theme was that working with other agencies had led to a "widening of perspective" and a means of "looking at other ways of working" which officers found beneficial and thought-provoking.

Only CPU officers felt that working in the Units could enhance their prospects for promotion.

12.4 DIFFICULT ASPECTS OF THE WORK

12.4.1 Heavy work load

All the officers felt that the Units had a very heavy workload. Several Units are stretched to capacity and officers are finding it difficult to deal with all incoming enquiries.

In all Forces, officers felt that they were getting child abuse enquiries that did not always require a specialist involvement. They attributed this to two related factors. Firstly, because most referrals come direct from social workers, bypassing police channels, other officers are not always aware of the volume of work undertaken in the Units. As a result, uniformed police pass all of their enquiries involving children to the specialist officers. Officer 11 felt this was due to a certain naivety on the part of these officers,

> "When we tell them we work in the Unit, they say 'Oh, you'll no be busy then', and send us all the minor little cases that they could deal with themselves."

The following comments further illustrate the tendency to indiscriminately pass on work to the Units,

> "Our colleagues on the shift don't appreciate what we do, nor the extent of our workload. Because of that they are not as supportive as they could be." (Officer 14)

> "I feel that some of the things we get in here could be screened a bit better. Some don't require specialist involvement. We get them though because we are here. And once we get them we have to do them." (Officer 10)

CID officers are also responsible for directing work to the Unit,

> "We are just the mice in the corner as far as the CID are concerned. We just want to get on with our work and they get us doing other things." (Officer 6)

The second reason for Units having a higher workload is because other officers are reluctant to deal with such cases, particularly child abuse cases.

> "A lot of officers wouldn't touch this sort of stuff with a barge-pole - especially the older ones ... Even officers that are above us in rank say 'well, it's up to you to decide things, you are the ones that know that sort of thing.'" (Officer 10)

> "A lot of them don't bother to find out how they would go about doing an enquiry because they don't feel it's their duty anymore. And they probably wouldn't know what to do. They would probably just get in a panic and phone the Unit for some guidance. That happens a lot. Not that they are being bolshie or wanting to pass the buck, it's just that they genuinely haven't dealt with such cases before because we are here." (Officer 4)

All specialist officers felt that they had taken over a substantial amount of work previously undertaken by uniformed and CID officers.

All officers said they did much more (unpaid) overtime since being seconded,

> "I was in here until 1am the other night - I was supposed to get off at 3pm. At least when you are on shift, another shift comes on at 3pm and you get away. In here you have to stay and finish what you are doing. I know a lot of officers do that, but it's more regular in the Unit." (Officer 4)

All officers felt their Units were under-staffed. Fourteen of the eighteen officers also felt that Units needed to provide twenty four hour cover.

12.4.2 Relations with rest of force

Another difficulty concerns the way that the work of the Units is viewed by other officers in the Force. Mention has already been made of the derogatory names by which the Units are known. Two thirds of officers felt that their work was seen as low priority within the police. They were concerned that it lacked credibility in the eyes of other officers. Similarly, they felt they got little recognition from their colleagues for their work, which they felt was demanding and often difficult. Most felt that this was because other officers were largely unaware of the volume and nature of the work. Some felt it was because they were closely associated with social workers.

Officers in two Units did, however, feel that their general credibility was growing. This, they felt, was due to the fact that they were having increasingly more contact with other officers, and also because they had begun to give talks and lectures to them.

12.4.3 Organisational issues

Officers maintained that the most difficult and stressful aspects of the work were not particularly related to the substantive nature of sexual assault and child abuse enquiries. Frustrations and difficulties were associated more with organisational and practical issues. Officer 8 summed up this view,

> "It is not the actual work that stresses me, it's the way it gets managed. Trying to organise an investigation is much more stressful than dealing with a nasty child abuse."

Common organisational difficulties cited by specialist officers included:

(i) **Arranging medical examinations**: this included the protracted length of time spent waiting for a police surgeon to become available; lack of female police surgeons; transporting victims over long distances to be medically examined.

(ii) **Facilities**: a lack of suitable interview and/or medical examination facilities; lack of vehicles; transportation problems were all mentioned.

(iii) **Working hours**: co-ordinating with social workers who work different hours was a particular concern.

(iv) **Paperwork**: the volume of paperwork and deadlines for its completion caused problems for most officers. A lack of clerical/secretarial support staff was felt to exacerbate this problem.

Although three quarters of officers stated that they enjoyed working in the Units, four said that they did not enjoy the work at all and were looking forward to their period of secondment coming to an end. All officers identified the organisational frustrations and delays outlined above as the main source of their frustration. One officer found the work itself rewarding and would prefer to "deal with a nasty child abuse case rather than a road traffic accident, any day", but said that the organisational problems associated with "trying to get the work done" made the work "an absolute nightmare job."

Frustrations also stemmed from the difficulties in obtaining corroboration in sexual assault and child abuse cases. Half of the officers (9) reported experiencing extreme frustration at some time when they were unable to obtain sufficient evidence for a prosecution. As one officer pointed out,

> " I could scream when that happens. Sometimes it can be so difficult to get the evidence. But when the child can't or won't speak, there is nothing we can do. We do send everything to the Fiscal, even hearsay evidence, but sometimes it's hopeless." (Officer 2)

Other officers also referred to the frustrations of a case going to court and ending in an acquittal.

> "I know I am not supposed to, but sometimes I feel let down by the criminal justice system. I think most women are let down by it. 'Not proven' acquittals are the worst - after all that has happened to her and after all the work we have put in - and you know he did it." (Officer 6)

12.4.4 Work-related stress and access to counselling

A minority of officers did identify feeling stressed at some stage while working in the Units. Although two officers said they had been on a stress management course, most officers have very limited access to counselling or support services within the Force. It was repeatedly stated that "police officers are not supposed to feel stressed" yet clearly some do. Official support mechanisms are seen as "laughable", "just a joke" and, most off-putting to officers "totally unconfidential."

> "If you have the feeling that you are sliding over the edge, you have nowhere to go. If you go to the police welfare officer, he will just phone your boss immediately, so it is not confidential. And your boss will call you in and it'll be a black mark against your name." (Officer 2)

Eight officers reported that they felt they had undergone some personal change since working in the Units. Typically, this was due to "increased paranoia" or "feelings of suspicion" about potential child abusers. For example, Officer 13 described how much more aware she had become of any bruising or injuries on children, even her own nieces and nephews. Officer 3 described how, when she is off-duty, she always has "half an eye open" when around children.

12.5   CONCLUSION

Specialist officers gave a range of views about their work in the Units. Overall, they saw the existence of the Units as an improvement in the police handling of sexual assault and child abuse. They acknowledged the range of skills required by officers in the Units and noted that both types of offences called for a different police response.

Although officers confirmed their primary role in the gathering of evidence, they also drew attention to their important role in offering support and care to victims. This is a role which provides them with a new perspective on policing.

They also noted organisational factors which constrained their work and the stress that it could entail.

CHAPTER 13

CONCLUSION

The research set out to provide a descriptive overview of the responses in each Scottish police Force to calls for changes in the investigation of violent crime against women and children. It did not have an evaluative function; nor did it have a remit to provide a consumer view of the changes which have occurred. Despite these limitations, however, the research addresses themes which are common to all Forces and it identifies positive aspects of the changes in investigative practice. It also points to areas where further improvements could be made.

This chapter considers the main themes to emerge from the research. It confirms the positive aspects of the Units, raises issues for policy-makers and identifies opportunities for further improvements in the police response. There are a number of areas in which significant change has occurred in the investigation of violent crime against women and children. These are considered below.

13.1 VICTIM-CENTRED INVESTIGATIONS

The welfare of victims has a higher priority in police investigations than a decade ago. It is now less likely for a complainer to have to repeat her allegation to several officers, the investigation is conducted more quickly, only the most essential procedures are carried out in the initial stages and more detailed questioning takes place once the victim has rested. In child abuse investigations police have improved their interviewing style and skills and they have become more concerned with child protection. In some Forces change has come about as a result of organisational factors; in others improvements are due to the effort and commitment of individual officers and their social work counterparts. The considerable diversity within and between Forces in the police response to sexual assault and child abuse means that the experience of victims varies . It is important to note that child abuse investigations require skills in dealing with children and in conducting difficult investigations.

13.2 TRAINED OFFICERS

In most Forces training has improved. A greater emphasis on formal training which includes a range of topics, methods and participants has produced investigating officers who are more empathic to the needs of victims. They have a better understanding of the impact of violence on women and children and there is now less emphasis in interviews on the credibility of victims.

Examples of good practice in training include: skills-based input, the long-term effects of sexual abuse on children, the emotional effects of sexual assault and the challenging of professional stereotypes. There are a number of areas which could be developed further:

(i) the organisation of training so that specialist officers and social workers from the same geographical area are trained together;

(ii) consideration of the appointment of staff who could co-ordinate inter-agency training in sexual assault and/or child abuse;

(iii) the provision of more training on interviewing children, especially those with physical or communication difficulties;

(iv) an extension of the 'aide' and 'exchange' systems;

(v) the expansion of specialist training to all uniformed and detective officers;

(vi) training in issues relating to domestic violence should be organised prior to any proposed role for specialist officers in this area.

13.3 DEDICATED FACILITIES

The establishment of specialist Units has provided a clear indication that the police have changed their approach to the issue of violence against women and children. The facilities offered to victims provide, for the most part, a secure and private environment in which they can begin to recover from their experiences. The Units' resources are adequate but in some Forces they will not be able to accommodate any increase in workload. There are also a number of issues relating to their location and resources:

(i) the relative merits of locating Units in the community or police stations need further exploration;

(ii) arrangements for medical examinations could be further improved;

(iii) the provision of designated secretarial and administrative resources to the Units would ease the burden on specialist officers. This would also ensure that there is a continuous presence in the Unit during office hours;

(iv) the allocation of vehicles for the exclusive use of the Units could ease the transportation of victims and make routine tasks outwith the Units easier to complete.

13.4 THE REMIT OF THE UNITS

The rapid growth and change undergone by Units in recent years indicates that police Forces are able to assimilate new concepts and policies and rapidly implement them. Increased levels of reporting has resulted in the Units being stretched to capacity. There are implications here for the future and some options for consideration include:

(i) an overall increase in resources to meet any increased demand;

(ii) a separation of roles and functions into two Units; one dealing with child abuse and the other with violent and/or sexual crime against women;

(iii) a shift in emphasis to a consultative role for the Units;

(iv) the development of techniques to differentiate between cases where a specialist response is needed and where a 'routine' response would suffice;

(v) the expansion of specialist training to all operational officers.

13.5 WOMEN OFFICERS

Chapter 6 noted that the Units are mainly staffed by female officers. There are a number of issues to be explored in this respect:

(i) the assumption that women officers are "the best for the job" because they are female may need to be challenged:

(ii) the implications of work in the Units being seen as 'women's work', leading to a lowering of morale and status for the work;

(iii) research to establish the career paths of female officers allocated to the Units to determine whether they offer the possibility of career advancement.

13.6 PROVISION OF INFORMATION TO VICTIMS

Information to victims about the progress of investigations remains patchy and leaves room for improvement. Suggestions for further consideration include:

(i) advice and information sheets outlining the process of an investigation with specific information on each stage to be given to every victim;

(ii) regular contact by letter or telephone for the duration of the investigation with the specialist investigating officer;

(iii) an official letter to the victim confirming the outcome of the case, rather than leaving the conveying of information to the discretion of the investigating officer;

(iv) The provision of up-to-date written information about local agencies offering support and advice to women and children who have experienced violence.

13.7 PUBLICITY

Chapter 5 noted difficulties for members of the public trying to contact their local Unit. An ongoing programme of publicity which incorporates a range of methods could be developed. It might include:

(i) a series of posters advertising and explaining the work of the Unit;

(ii) posters, leaflets and information on specific issues eg. the role of the specialist Unit, investigating officer, police surgeon;

(iii) a full list of the names and addresses of Units throughout Scotland to be available for widespread distribution;

(iv) an entry for the Unit in every local phonebook;

(v) An ongoing series of talks and presentations about the work of the Unit.

13.8 LINKS WITH OTHER AGENCIES

This is another area where experience varies from Force to Force. Relationships between the police and the Procurator Fiscal and Reporter to the Children's Panel have improved on both an agency and individual basis. Relationships with police surgeons vary and the impetus for any change may need to come from them rather than from the police.

Chapter 11 outlined how working relationships with social workers vary, depending on the degree and extent of joint working. One area for further investigation is the extent to which the 'degree of jointness' in working arrangements affects outcome in terms of the number of interviews and medical examinations carried out and the quality of evidence gathered in the investigation.

Opportunities for improvements include:
  (i)   more joint training with staff who will be working together on investigations;
  (ii) regular inter-agency meetings to update other agencies about the work of the Units and discuss specific problems and common concerns;
  (iii) the inclusion of voluntary support organisations in police training courses.

13.9   ORGANISATIONAL ISSUES

Chapters 5 and 8 drew attention to the organisational issues which have influenced the development of the Units. Their internal command structure, the designation of seconded officers with detective status and the methods for seconding officers to the Units are all important factors. Developments for the future might include:

  (i)   the appointment of a promoted post (Unit Sergeant) who would take responsibility for the day-to-day running of the Unit and provide a direct channel for officers to make requests or discuss problems;
  (ii) an agreed and fixed period of secondment to the Units;
  (iii) some degree of choice for officers about working in the Units;
  (iv) regular supervision and support for the work which acknowledges its stressful nature;
  (v)   a system which provides some overlap between shifts;
  (vi) a review of the working hours of the Units.

13.10 ISSUES FOR POLICY-MAKERS

Specialist Units may not be cost-effective in the accepted fiscal sense of the term. They entail additional expenditure and staff deployment and they may offer little in the way of staff or resource savings. They do, however, offer 'value for money' in other ways, including a more positive view of the police in a sensitive area of policing, improved relationships with other agencies, a means for improving the quality of evidence, smoother investigations, an overall reduction in personnel engaged in investigations, the reduction of repetitive questioning and increased job satisfaction for those who work in the Units. Police believe that they provide an improved comprehensive service to victims.

Whilst several Forces have updated their Force Orders since inception this could be done on a more systematic and regular basis. It will also be important for updates to take account of new initiatives and relevant research findings.

The way ahead for the Units is not yet clear. The various examples described in this Report all have their strengths and weaknesses. Some questions present themselves for consideration in the development of the Units:

1   How appropriate is it to deal with sexual assault, child abuse and, possibly, domestic violence in the same Unit?

2   How can the existence and work of the Units be more effectively communicated within the Force to other police officers?

3   What is the need for better co-ordination between Forces on policies for dealing with sexual assault and child abuse?

4   Are the Units, by their very existence, indirectly contributing to the marginalisation of violence against women and children as an area of public and police concern?

5   Do specialist Units have a temporary or permanent role in relation to mainstream police and social work?

6   Should domestic violence be incorporated into the work of the Units?

7   Can the means be found to improve communication between Units and voluntary organisations who can provide feedback on 'customer-satisfaction'?

8   What is the scope for improving and/or standardising training for work in the Units?

9   What can be done to enhance the status of Unit officers?

10 What is the optimum period of secondment for officers to the Units?

These questions will merit discussion in the near future and further research will be needed to evaluate the outcome of the next phase of the Units' development and, equally importantly, the views of women and children who use them.

APPENDIX 1

SCOTTISH POLICE FORCES

Following the reorganisation of Scottish local government in May 1975[1], the police in Scotland were restructured into eight separate Forces (see Map). Although each Force has the same basic internal structure and organisation, they vary significantly in terms of size of Force area, the population they serve, staffing, resources and crime statistics. A short summary of facts relating to each Force confirms this variation.

Dumfries and Galloway Police covers a wide and dispersed rural area on the south-west border. It has a population of approximately 148,000 and the main towns are Dumfries and Stranraer. It is the smallest police Force in Britain and in December 1991 had 370 officers deployed in four Divisions.

Strathclyde Police covers a very large area of the Scottish mainland and includes several islands. It has a population of 2,306,000, almost half of Scotland's total population. The population is concentrated in the greater Glasgow area and many large towns throughout the Force area. Strathclyde is the second largest police Force in Britain (next to the Metropolitan Police) with a total of 6,735 officers deployed in 15 territorial Divisions.

Lothian and Borders Police encompasses the south eastern corner of Scotland. It a serves a large population of almost 853,000 concentrated in the city of Edinburgh and several other large towns. In December 1991, there were 2,470 officers deployed in six Divisions.

Central Scotland Police is located between the Forth and Clyde estuaries. It has a population of approximately 272,000 concentrated in Stirling and other major towns. In December 1991 there were 636 officers deployed in two territorial Divisions.

Fife Constabulary covers the smallest Force area in Scotland a population of approximately 346,000. It has a rural/urban mix of coastal towns and cultivated farmland. In December 1991 there were 775 officers deployed in three territorial Divisions.

Tayside Police covers a medium sized area with a population of 394,000 concentrated in the cities of Dundee and Perth. In December 1991, there were 1,047 officers which are deployed in three territorial Divisions.

Grampian Police covers a large area with a population of approximately 506,000 concentrated in the city of Aberdeen. The landward area is predominantly rural. In December 1991, there were 1,134 officers deployed in three territorial Divisions.

Northern Constabulary covers a large area of mainland and islands, the greatest landmass of any British Force. It has a population of approximately 277,000. Most of the Force area is sparsely populated, although the majority of people reside in and around Inverness and Dingwall. Parts of the Force area are very remote. There are 3 large territorial Divisions and in December 1991 there were 654 officers.

SCOTTISH POLICE AREAS

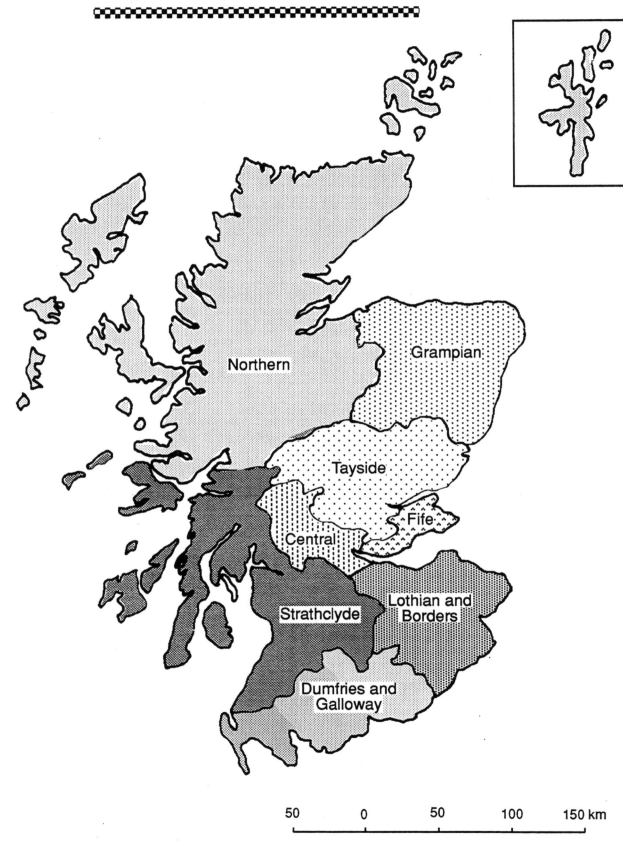

Northern

Grampian

Tayside

Fife

Central

Strathclyde

Lothian and Borders

Dumfries and Galloway

50   0   50   100   150 km

Table A.1   Crimes reported in 1991

Police Force	Total Crimes reported	Group 2 * Crimes in 1991 (A)	Cruel and unnatural treatment of children (B)	(A) and (B) as % of total crimes reported
Dumfries & Galloway	25,956	118	23	0.54
Strathclyde	51,6293	2,918	581	0.67
Lothian & Borders	16,1992	897	142	0.64
Central	25,028	216	108	1.29
Fife	58,342	338	86	0.72
Tayside	84,089	403	123	0.62
Grampian	88,814	757	101	0.96
Northern	36,877	197	78	0.74

Source: Chief Constables' Annual Reports, 1991

Notes

The figures in this table have been drawn from official criminal statistics of crimes made known to the police and are to be used as a guide only. Official criminal statistics of crimes made known to police are not the same as criminal incidents that are reported and defined as such by the public. This category includes cases which, after an enquiry or investigation, are recorded as crimes by the police.

* Group 2 crimes include, incest, rape, assault with intent to rape/ravish, indecent assault, lewd and libidinous practices, indecent exposure, age related homosexual offences, unlawful behaviour with girls under 16, prostitution.

Footnotes

---

1   Local Government (Scotland) Act 1973.

APPENDIX 2

SPECIALIST UNITS/OFFICERS IN SCOTTISH POLICE FORCES

CENTRAL

Central Police
Child Protection Unit
Bannockburn Police Office
Bannockburn
STIRLING
Telephone 0786 813412
Has Force-wide remit

DUMFRIES AND GALLOWAY

Dumfries and Galloway Police
Female and Child Unit
Police Headquarters
Loreburn Street
DUMFRIES
DG1 1HP
Telephone 0387 52112
Has Force-wide remit

FIFE

Child Protection Unit
The Lodge House
Priory Lane
DUNFERMLINE
Fife
Telephone 0383 724074
Covers Dunfermline, Cowdenbeath and Dalgety Bay areas of Fife.

Child Protection Unit
c/o Social Work Department
East Albert Road
KIRKCALDY
Fife
Telephone 0592 264747
Covers remainder of Force area

GRAMPIAN

Grampian Police
Female & Child Enquiry Unit
Police Headquarters
Queen Street
ABERDEEN
AB9 1BA
Telephone 0224 639111

Grampian Police
Female & Child Enquiry Unit
"A" Division Headquarters
Moray Street
ELGIN
Moray
Telephone 0343 543101

Grampian Police
Female & Child Enquiry Unit
Merchant Street
PETERHEAD
Banff
Buchan
Telephone 0779 72571

LOTHIAN AND BORDERS

Lothian & Borders Police
Women and Child Unit
"B" Division Headquarters
St Leonards Street
EDINBURGH
Telephone 031 662-5000
Covers central city area.

Lothian & Borders Police
Women and Child Unit
"E" Division Headquarters
Newbattle Road
DALKEITH
EH22 3AX
Telephone 031 663-2855
Covers East Lothian and eastern area of city

Lothian & Borders Police
Women and Child Unit
"F" Division Headquarters
Almondvale South
LIVINGSTON
EH54 6NB
Telephone 0506 31200
Covers West Lothian, South Queensferry, Kirkliston, Balerno, Currie, Ratho, Livingston and Bathgate.

Lothian & Borders Police
Women and Child Unit
"G" Division Headquarters
Wilton Hill
HAWICK
TD9 8BA
Telephone 0450 75051 Ext 4447
Covers districts of Ettrick & Lauderdale, Berwickshire, Roxburgh and Tweedale, Hawick, Galashiels, Jedburgh, Selkirk, Kelso, Newton St Boswells and Duns.

NORTHERN

Northern Constabulary
Child Abuse Co-ordinator
Community Involvement Department
The Castle
INVERNESS
IV2 3EG
Telephone 0463 239191

STRATHCLYDE

Strathclyde Police
Female and Child Unit
"A" Division Headquarters
50 Stewart Street
Glasgow
Telephone 041 332 1113
Covers city centre.

Strathclyde Police
Female and Child Unit
"B" Division Headquarters
50 Montrose Street
Clydebank
Glasgow
Telephone 041 941 1113
Covers West End of Glasgow - Partick, Garscadden, Drumchapel and Clydebank.

Strathclyde Police
Female and Child Unit
"C" Division Headquarters
1380 Maryhill Road
Glasgow
Telephone 041 946 1113
Covers North and West parts of the city - Milngavie, Bearsden, Maryhill, Temple,Saracen, Kelvindale, North Kelvinside, Anniesland, Knightswood, Possil and Ruchill.

Strathclyde Police
Female and Child Unit
"D" Division Headquarters
6 Baird Street
Glasgow
Telephone 041 552 6333
Covers North East Glasgow district and Strathkelvin district - Kirkintillock, Bishopbriggs and Easterhouse.

Strathclyde Police
Female and Child Unit
"E" Division Headquarters
851 London Road
Glasgow
Telephone 041 554 1113
Covers the East end of the City - Bridgeton, Calton, Dalmarnock, Dennistoun, Shettleston, Barlanark, Carntyne, Greenfield, Parkhead, Springboig, Bailleston, Garrowhill, Mount Vernon, Broomhouse and Carlyle.

Strathclyde Police
Female and Child Unit
"F" Division Headquarters
744 Aitkenhead Road
Glasgow
Telephone 041 442 1113
Covers South of the City - Pollockshaws, Castlemilk, Rutherglen, Mount Florida, East Pollokshields, Queens Park and Crosshill.

Strathclyde Police
Female and Child Unit
"G" Division Headquarters
18 Orkney Street
Glasgow
Telephone 041 445 1113
Covers South side of the Clyde - Govan, Pollok, Priesthill, Darnley, South Nitshill, Carnwadric, Clarkston, Giffnock, Newton Mearns, Eastwood.

Strathclyde Police
Female and Child Unit
"K" Division Headquarters
Mill Street
Paisley
Telephone No 041 889 1113
Covers Paisley, Johnstone, Renfrew, Barrhead, Elderslie, Linwood, Bridge of Weir, Lochwinnoch, Erskine and Langbank.

Strathclyde Police
Female and Child Unit
"L" Division Headquarters
Stirling Road
Overtoun
Dumbarton
Telephone 0389 63311

Argyll and Bute district - Oban, Dunoon, Rothesay, Campbeltown, Dumbarton, Helensburgh, Alexandria, Lochgilphead, Mull, Islay and Jura.

Strathclyde Police
Female and Child Unit
"N" Division Headquarters
Whittington Street
Coatbridge
Telephone 0236 20155
Covers Monklands, Coatbridge, Cumbernauld, Kilsyth and Airdrie.

Strathclyde Police
Female and Child Unit
"P" Division Headquarters
217 Windmillhill Street
Motherwell
Telephone 0698 66144
Covers Motherwell, Wishaw, Bellshill and Shotts.

Strathclyde Police
Female and Child Unit
"Q" Division Headquarters
Campbell Street
Hamilton
Telephone 0698 286303
Covers East Kilbride, Hamilton, Clydesdale, Lanark, Blantyre, Uddingston, Larkhall, Strathaven, Chapelton, Biggar, Abington, Leadhills, Carluke, Crawford and Law.

Strathclyde Police
Female and Child Unit
"R" Division Headquarters
1 King Street
Ayr
Telephone 0292 266966
Covers Kyle and Carrick districts and Cumnock district - Ayr, Troon, Girvan and Prestwick.

Strathclyde Police
Female and Child Unit
"U" Division Headquarters
10 St Marnock Street
Kilmarnock
Telephone 0563 21188

Covers Kilmarnock, Cunninghame, Loudon, Irvine, Saltcoats, Stewarton, Kilmaurs, Fenwick, Dunlop, Darvel, Kilwinning, Ardrossan, Largs, Arran, Great Cumbrae.

Strathclyde Police
Female and Child Unit
"X" Division Headquarters
160 Rue End Street
Greenock
Telephone 0475 24444
Covers Inverclyde district - Greenock, Port Glasgow, Gourock, Kilmacolm and Wemyss Bay.

TAYSIDE

Tayside Police
Child and Female Specialist Enquiry Section
West Bell Street
DUNDEE
DD1 9JU
Telephone 0382 23200
Covers Central City area and immediate environs.
There are "designated officers" in Eastern and Western division, but no "Unit" as such.

Tayside Police
Child and Female Specialist Enquiry Section
Barrack Street
PERTH
PH1 5SF
Telephone 0738 21141
Covers Perth and Kinross District - Perth, Blairgowrie, Crieff, Pitlochry, Abernethy, Bankfoot, Bridge of Earn,
Methven, Kinloch Rannoch and Aberfeldy.

Tayside Police
Child and Female Specialist Enquiry Section
East High Street
FORFAR
Angus
DD8 1BP
Telephone 0307 62551
Covers Angus District - Forfar, Arbroath, Montrose, Kirriemuir, Glamis and Carnoustie.

APPENDIX 3

SPECIALIST OFFICERS: BIOGRAPHICAL DATA

	Sex	Age	Length of Service (years)	Time in Unit (years)
Officer 1	F	30	12	2
Officer 2	F	25	6	1
Officer 3	F	27	9	1
Officer 4	F	30	5	3
Officer 5	F	26	6	2
Officer 6	F	27	4	2
Officer 7	F	26	7	3
Officer 8	F	27	8	3
Officer 9	M	31	13	2
Officer 10	F	28	8	3
Officer 11	F	27	9	3
Officer 12	F	24	6	3 months
Officer 13	F	27	9	2
Officer 14	F	26	6	1
Officer 15	F	38	19	2
Officer 16	F	30	12	4
Officer 17	F	28	8	1
Officer 18	F	34	13	3

CRU RESEARCH - RECENTLY PUBLISHED WORK

Partnership in the Regeneration of Urban Scotland: (HMSO) (1996)

The Safer Cities Programme in Scotland - Evaluation of Safe Greater Easterhouse: Dr James K Carnie. (1996) (£5.00)

The Safer Cities Programme in Scotland - Evaluation of Dundee (North East): Dr James K Carnie. (1996) (£5.00)

The Safer Cities Programme in Scotland - Evaluation of Safe Castlemilk: Dr James K Carnie. (1996) (£5.00)

The Safer Cities Programme in Scotland - Overview Report: Dr James K Carnie. (1996) (£5.00)

Does Closed Circuit Television Prevent Crime?: Emma Short and Dr Jason Ditton, Scottish Centre for Criminology. (1996) (£2.50)

Evaluation of Speedwatch: System Three Scotland. (1996) (£5.00)

Proactive Policing - An Evaluation of the Central Scotland Police Crime Management Model: Peter Amey, Chris Hale and Steve Uglow (Canterbury Business School, University of Kent). (1996) (£5.00)

The Pedestrian Casualty Problem in Scotland: Why So Many?: Gordon Harland and Derek Halden, Transport Research Laboratory. (1996) (£5.00)

Energy Conservation and Planning: Howard Liddell, Drew Mackie and Gillian Macfarlane (GAIA Planning Consultants). (1996) (£5.00)

The Speeding Driver: Colin Buchanan & Partners. (1996) (£5.00)

Foreign Language Interpreters in the Scottish Criminal Courts: The MVA Consultancy. (1996) (£5.00)

Grounds of Appeal in Criminal Cases: Dr Peter Duff and Frazer McCallum, Law Faculty, Aberdeen University. (1996) (£7.00 from HMSO)

Assessment of the Implications of Radium Contamination of Dalgety Bay Beach and Foreshore: Dr B Heaton, Prof F Glasser, Miss S Jones, Dr N Bonney, Mr A Glendinning, Dr D Sell (University of Aberdeen and Auris Environmental Ltd). (1996) (£10.00)

Scoping Study on Rural Development Issues in Scotland: Pollyanna Chapman, Ed Conway and Mark Shucksmith (Arkleton Centre for Rural Development Research, Aberdeen University). (1996) (£5.00)

Living in Rural Scotland: A Study of Life in Four Rural Communities: Karen MacNee, Central Research Unit. (HMSO) (1996) (£10.00)

Services in Rural Scotland: MacKay Consultants. (HMSO) (1996) (£10.00)

Listening to Victims of Crime: M D MacLeod, R G W Prescott and L Carson (School of Psychology, University of St Andrews). (1996) (£6.00)

Estimating the Prevalence of Drug Misuse in Scotland: Dr Martin Frischer, SCIEH. (1996) (£5.00)

Accidents at Signal Controlled Junctions and Pelican Crossings in Glasgow: Halcrow Fox. (1996) (£5.00)

Housing for Young People in Ferguslie Park: The MVA Consultancy. (1996) (£5.00)

Scottish Rural Life Update: A Revised Socio-Economic Profile of Rural Scotland: Nick Williams, Mark Shucksmith, Helen Edmond and Andy Gemmell, University of Aberdeen. (1996) (£10.00)

An Evaluation of GRO Grants for Owner Occupation: Keith Kintrea, Kenneth Gibb, Christian Hermansen, Margaret Keoghan, Moira Munro and Alan McGregor, Centre for Housing Research and Urban Studies, University of Glasgow. (1996) (£10.00)

Opening Up Dialogue: Dr J Curran, The Scottish Office Home Department - Central Research Unit. (1996) (free publication)

Gyle Impact Study: Roger Tym & Partners in association with Oscar Faber TPA. (1996) (£15.00)

Main Findings from the 1993 Scottish Crime Survey: Simon Anderson and Susan Leitch. (1996) (£7.00)

New Ideas in Rural Development No 1: Promoting the Development of Effective Information and Advice Services for Rural Areas - A Framework For Action in Scotland: Juliet Harvey. (1996) (£2.50)

Evaluation of Young Driver Cinema Advert: System Three Scotland. (1996) (£5.00)

Water and Recreation: A Guide to Managing the Recreational Use of Water in Scotland: Cobhams Resource Consultants updated by Karen MacNee and Juliet Harvey. (1996) (£5.00)

Research Evaluation of Programmes for Violent Men: Russell Dobash, Rebecca Dobash, Kate Cavanagh and Ruth Lewis. (1996) (£6.00)

Estimating the Housing Needs of Community Care Groups: Moira Munro, Delia Lomax, Sharon Lancaster, Glen Bramley, Keith Anderson, School of Planning and Housing, Edinburgh College of Art/Heriot-Watt University. (1996) (£5.00)

The Use of the Compensation Order in Scotland: Jennifer Hamilton and Mik Wisniewski, University of Stirling. (1996) (£5.00)

Examining the Test: An Evaluation of the Police Standard Entrance Test: Valerie Wilson, Peter Glissov and Bridget Somekh, Scottish Council for Research in Education. (1996) (£5.00)

A Sentencing Information System for The Scottish High Court: Neil Hutton, Alan A Paterson, Cyrus Tata and John N Wilson, University of Strathclyde. (1996) (*£5.00*)

Linking Road Traffic Accident Statistics to Census Data in Lothian: Ibrahim M Abdalla, Robert Raeside and Derek Barker, Napier University. (1996) (*£5.00*)

Delivering Community Care: A Petch, J Cheetham, R Fuller, C MacDonald and F Myres with A Hallam and M Knapp (1996) (*£21.00*)

New Ideas in Rural Development No.2: Action on Scottish Rural Transport - Helping Local Communities Tackle Their Transport Problems: Stephanie Herbert, Central Research Unit. (1996) (*£2.50*)

Scottish Rural Transport Action Guide: Practical advice on how to address your community's transport needs: Stephanie Herbert, Central Research Unit. (1996) (*£5.00*)

Without Shelter: Estimating Rooflessness in Scotland: Ian Shaw, Michael Bloor and Stephen Roberts, School of Social Administration Studies, University of Wales, Cardiff. (1996) (*£5.00*)

Fiscal Fines: The Operation of Section 56 of the Criminal Justice (Scotland) Act 1987: Dr Peter Duff, Kenneth Meechan, Michael Christie and David Lessels, Aberdeen University. (1996) (*£5.00*).

Pathways to Welfare for Pakistani Elderly People in Glasgow: Alison Bowes and Naira Dar. (1996) (£5.00)

Readiness to Practise. The Training of Social Workers in Scotland and Their First Year in Work: John Triseliotis and Peter Marsh. (1996) (£5.00)

A Chance to Change: Any Intervention With Young People Who Have Sexually Abused Others. Maureen Buist and Roger Fuller. (1997) (£5.00)

Towards A Strategy for Vacant Land: Pieda, in association with The Turnbull Jeffrey Partnership Planning, Economic and Development Consultants. (1997) (*£5.00)*

Cash Incentive Schemes in Scotland: Richard Evans, Central Research Unit. (1996) (*£5.00*)

Research into Criminal Legal Aid Under Summary Proceedings in Scotland: A Review. Sue Warner, Central Research Unit. (1996) (*£5.00*)

Comparative Study of Local Authority Current Expenditure in Scotland, England and Wales: Report: Coopers & Lybrand and Pieda. (1997) (*£10.00*)

Comparative Study of Local Authority Current Expenditure in Scotland, England and Wales: Summary: Coopers & Lybrand and Pieda. (1997) (Free)

New Ideas in Rural Development No 3: Involving Rural Communities - The CADISPA Approach. Geoff Fagan, University of Strathclyde. (1997) (*£2.50*)

The Deterrent Effect of Enforcement in Road Safety - System Three. (1997) (*£5.00*)

Crime and Criminal Justice in Scotland: Peter Young, Centre for Law and Society, University of Edinburgh. (1996) (*£9.99*)

Local Authority Organisation and Management in Scotland 1975-1996: Richard Kerley with Mark Urquhart. (1997) (*£5.00*).

Transfers of Local Authority and Scottish Homes Housing: Tony Graham, Lorna Hamilton, Fiona Ballantyne and Caroline Caste, Organisational Development and Support Ltd. (1997) (*£5.00*)

Impact of the Road Network on Scotland's Accident Rates: The MVA Consultancy. (1997) (*£7.50*)

Nomination Arrangements in Scotland: Anne Yanetta, Hilary Third and Hal Pawson, School of Planning and Housing, Edinburgh College of Art/Heriot-Watt University. (1997) (*£7.50*)

The Use of Additional Capital Allocations for Homelessness Projects: An Evaluation: Sarah Dyer, Central Research Unit. (1997) (*£5.00*)

Local Authority Sites for Travellers: Anne Douglas. (1997) (*£5.00*)

New Tenants of Scottish Local Authorities: Jeremy Hardin, The MVA Consultancy. (1997) (*£5.00*)

Good Practice in Rural Development No 1: Effective Partnership Working: Bill Slee and Patrick Snowdon, Department of Agriculture, University of Aberdeen with Robert Gordon (Kilmartin Glen Project), Bill Marshall (Gordon Enterprise Trust) and Andrew Wells (Glenlivet Estate). (1997) (*£2.50*)

Mutual Consent Written Agreements in Family Law: Frances Wasoff, Ann McGuckin and Lilian Edwards, University of Edinburgh. (1997) (*£5.00*)

Survey of Family Business in the Scottish Courts: MVA Consultancy. (Research Findings only Available) (1997) (*£5.00*)

Socio-Legal Research in the Scottish Courts Volume 4: Diane Machin and Rebecca Sawyer. (1997) (*£5.00*)

A Study of Crime in rural Scotland: Simon Anderson, Social Research Unit, System Three. (1997) (*£10.00*)

Review of Opencast Coal Mining Operations in Scotland: RSK Environment Ltd. (1997) (*£5.00*)

Community Involvement and Rural Policy: John Bryden, Drennan Watson, Catherine Storey and Jeroen van Alphen. (1997) (*£2.50*)

Good Practice in Rural Development: No 2 Community Involvement in rural Development Initiatives: Rural Forum and Rural Research Branch. (1997) (*£2.50*)

The Range and Availability of Domiciliary Care Services in Scotland: Lia Curtice, Fiona Fraser and Tracy Leca. (1997) (*£6.00*)

Retailing and Small Shops: Andrew Smith and Leigh Sparks, Institute for Retail Studies, University of Stirling. (1997) (*£5.00*)

Multiply Deprived Households - A 1991 Census Based Analysis: Pauline Martin. (1997) (*£5.00*)

Preparing Child Witnesses for Court: Kathleen Murray, Centre for the study of the , University of Glasgow. (1997) (*£5.00*)

Contact and Complaint Handling by the Planning Service: Peter Gibson Associates. (1997) (*£5.00*)

Public Access to Planning Information: B M Illsley, M G Lloyd, B Lynch and V Burbridge, Centre for Planning Research, School of Town and Regional Planning, University of Dundee. (1997) (*£5.00*)

Quality Assessment in Development Control: Jeremy Rowan-Robinson and William Walton (Department of Land Economy, Aberdeen University), Roger Durman, Martin Drumond and Rachel Gee (Montagu Evans, Chartered Surveyors). (1997) (*£5.00*)

The Provision of Housing and Community Care in Rural Scotland: Janet Field and Christine Oldman, Centre for Housing Policy, University of York. (1997) (*£5.00*)

Dedicated Resources: Dedicated Responses. Evaluation of the Mental Illness Specific Grant. Bernadette Laffey and Alison Petch (1997) (*£6.00*)

A Guide to the Development of Services for Alcohol & Drug Misusers: R Yates (1997) (*£3.00*)

Expenditure on Criminal Legal Aid: Report on a Comparative Pilot Study of Scotland, England and Wales, and the Netherlands. Tamara Goriely, Cyrus Tata, Alan A Paterson, TPR Social & Legal Research Law School, University of Strathclyde. (1997) (*£5.00*)

Review of The Scottish Office Road Safety Research Programme 1989-1997: Janet Ruiz, Transport and Road Safety Research Branch. (1997) (*£2.50*)

New Ideas in Rural Development No 4 - Community Involvement in Small Scale Tourism Initiatives: Stephanie Herbert, Rural Research Branch. (1997) (*£2.50*)

Right to Buy Resales in Scotland: Hal Pawson, Craig Watkins and James Morgan, School of Planning and Housing, Edinburgh College of Art/Heriot Watt University. (1997) (*£7.50*)

Electronically printed by The Stationery Office 10/97